MW01006846

ROMEO
AND
JULIET

Juliet: O Romeo, Romeo! Wherefore art thou Romeo? *(ACT II, Scene 2)*

SHAKESPEARE ON STAGE

VOLUME 3

ROMEO
AND
JULIET

by
William Shakespeare

edited and illustrated by
Diane Davidson

SWAN BOOKS
FAIR OAKS, CALIFORNIA

Published by

SWAN BOOKS
P.O. Box 2498
Fair Oaks, California 95628

Printed in the United States of America

Library of Congress Cataloging in Publication Data

Shakespeare, William, 1564-1616.
    Romeo and Juliet.

    (Shakespeare on stage ; v. 3)
    I. Davidson, Diane. II. Title. III. Serie
Shakespeare, William, 1564-1616. Shakespeare
stage ; v. 3.
PR2878.R6D3 1983   822.3'3   83-12309
ISBN 0-934048-07-X
ISBN 0-934048-06-1 (pbk.)

To Helen

SHAKESPEARE ON STAGE

Vol. 1 *Macbeth*

Vol. 2 *Julius Caesar*

Vol. 3 *Romeo and Juliet*

Vol. 4 *The Merchant of Venice*

Vol. 5 *A Midsummer Night's Dream**

Vol. 6 *Hamlet, Prince of Denmark*

*Especially recommended for the young beginner.

FOREWORD TO THE SERIES

Sometimes, in our desire to appreciate Shakespeare properly, we forget the obvious: that Shakespeare was not a schoolteacher, not a classical scholar, but a professional entertainer. He made his chief living in the theatre as an actor and producer. There is no evidence that he helped his fellow-actors Heminge and Condell preserve his works in print for readers. The plays were written to be heard and seen.

Therefore, to me the printed words are only half of Shakespeare's true intent; the completed show is all. To remedy this situation somewhat for leisure readers, I prepared this adaption, cutting the text to suit an average audience, supplying the missing visual effects by descriptions, and adding explanatory notes in parentheses where necessary. The awkward ten-syllable printed line has been discarded, as it does not appear in a living theatre production. Shakespeare's words, however, are not changed. But my efforts thus are incomplete. The plays should also be read aloud with a group of friends, for Shakespeare's words feel good inside the mouth, and his sounds are a delight to any ear. A great writer should be enjoyed with all the senses.

I described my approach to a friend.

"But you're not really changing Shakespeare," he said. "You're just directing his shows on paper."

"Yes," I answered, "that's my intent — to give his spoken words a natural background."

Perhaps Will himself would not be too displeased. To his Elizabethan age, a play was play, not work.

x

And so I think it sensible at first for people to read shortened versions of Shakespeare's plays, with immediate explanations, in order to become familiar with the stories and major scenes. Also the reader begins to tune his ears to Shakespeare's speech. Later, we gain even more enjoyment from the uncut manuscripts and from different interpretations, especially on the stage. But however we approach Shakespeare's great plays, we should take pleasure in them.

Diane Davidson

Fair Oaks, California
1979

ROMEO
AND
JULIET

CHARACTERS

The Ruling Family

> Escalus, Prince of Verona
> Mercutio, kinsman to the Prince and friend to
> Romeo, the quicksilver wit and clown of the
> young men's group
> Paris, a pleasant young Count or "County," kins-
> man to the Prince and suitor to Juliet

The House of Montague

> Montague, a nobleman
> Lady Montague, his wife
> Romeo, their romantic young son
> Benvolio, Romeo's cousin and steady friend
> Balthasar, servant to Romeo
> Abram, servant to Montague

The House of Capulet

> Old Capulet, a hot-tempered noble
> Lady Capulet, his young wife
> Juliet, their beautiful, clear-minded daughter
> Tybalt, the Capulets' young nephew, sleek and
> deadly
> Nurse, a jolly middle-aged servant to Juliet
> Peter, a stupid servant
> Old Man, cousin to Capulet
> Sampson ⎫
> Gregory ⎬ servants to Capulet

The Clergy

Friar Lawrence, a kindly old Franciscan priest
Friar John, a younger brother

Others

Chorus, the announcer of the Prologue
Apothecary, a medieval druggist
Officer and Watchmen, the local police
Three Musicians
Citizens of Verona, Gentlefolk, Maskers, Torch-
bearers, Pages, Guards, Servants, and Atten-
dants

THE BACKGROUND
OF THE PLAY

In *Romeo and Juliet*, probably Shakespeare's most famous tragic romance, the events seem both strange and familiar to us. Old noble families feud. Groups of rich young men prowl the streets, playing jokes, gate-crashing fashionable parties, and dueling at the slightest excuse. Girls of thirteen are ready for marriage. Headlong love and sudden death are natural. And beautiful young lovers die. To the last, we ask the eternal "Why?"

At the beginning of the play, the Prologue tells us that Romeo and Juliet are "star-crossed," cursed by fate to love and perish, according to their astrological signs. And to some extent this is true: accident or luck decides their meeting at the Capulet ball, at a time when Romeo is already in love with another girl, Rosaline; bad luck and hasty tempers cause the fatal Mercutio-Tybalt duel and Romeo's banishment; and unhappy fortune makes Juliet awaken from her drugged sleep a few minutes too late to prevent Romeo's suicide.

But why does their bad luck exist? To this question Shakespeare suggests a medieval answer in one of Romeo's first speeches on love: "Why then, O brawling love! O loving hate! O anything of nothing first create! O heavy lightness! Serious vanity! Misshapen chaos of well-seeming forms! Feather of lead, bright smoke,

cold fire, sick health!..." Here Romeo does more than quibble in the fashionable style of Petrarch. He describes the world composed of contradictions, of opposites, a theme that Shakespeare developed to its fullest in *Macbeth*. The basis for this idea lies in the nature of the world, which was created out of nothing — out of Chaos — and retains to a large extent its chaotic character, causing accidents, good luck and bad luck, and irregularities of fortune. And man's duty, Shakespeare implies, is to establish justice, dependabilitiy, peace, law, discipline — all the godly attributes that shape raw chaos into civilization, an outlook shared by many other Elizabethans.

But natural accident causes only part of the fatal concourse of events; the rest arises from the uncontrolled natures of the characters, both young and old.

The greatest human error in the play is that of the very young: hastiness. Romeo and Juliet meet, fall in love, marry, separate and die — all in the space of five days. In that time, they try to grow up too fast. True, they mature, through experience of love and sorrow, but they pay a terrible price for uncontrolled love.

The adults also bring about the tragedy by failing to fulfill the responsibilities of their positions. The Prince fails to stop the feud. The Nurse and Friar fail to tell the parents of the budding romance. The Montagues and Capulets cannot control the members of their houses. In the end, the fathers grow disciplined also, declaring peace over the dead bodies of their young.

Yet proper use of medieval law would have solved all difficulties in this story. If Romeo and Juliet had thought of appealing to the Prince, going over the heads of their parents to a higher authority, their marriage would have been welcomed as an alliance of the feuding families, completely in line with the Prince's policy of civic peace. This legal move was used to solve parental disapproval in Shakespeare's *Midsummer Night's Dream,* written about the same time. Yet in *Romeo and Juliet,* the Prince cannot approve of the marriage as he does not hear of it until it is too late. The lovers do not inform him of their plans, for they are too young to realize such advantages. The Nurse is too earthy to consider legal solutions, and the Friar is too unworldly. The one person who knows both the lovers and the Prince — Mercutio, the Prince's cousin and Romeo's quick-witted friend — is accidently slain moments after Romeo's secret wedding, so that his potential help is lost.

Thus, it is not only the chaos of the stars but the inner chaos of humanity that brings about misfortune for Romeo and Juliet. But although the underlying themes run deep, in the end it is Shakespeare's people and poetry that we remember, in this tale of passionate young lovers doomed to die.

ACT I

Scene 1

(In front of the stage curtain comes a character masked like a member of a Greek Chorus. He speaks the Prologue, telling the main events of the story. As he introduces the scene, the curtains part to show a sun-drenched plaza in Verona, Italy, where two magnificent town houses face each other across a fountain in the center. These mansions belong to the Montagues and the Capulets, who have a long-standing feud with many deaths on both sides.)

Chorus: Two households, both alike in dignity, in fair Verona, where we lay our scene, from ancient grudge break to new mutiny, where civil blood makes civil hands unclean.

(The Chorus announces the love and suicide of the children of the two houses.) From forth the fatal loins of these two foes, a pair of star-crossed lovers take their life. *(The story of their romance and the conflict of their families, a conflict which only the lovers' deaths resolve, is the subject of the brief play.)* The fearful passage of their death-marked love, and the continuance of their parents' rage, which, but their children's end, naught could remove, is now the two hours' traffic of our stage.

(If the audience is patient, the Chorus promises the actors will try to correct their faults.) The which, if you with patient ears attend, what here shall miss, our toil shall strive to mend.

(As the Chorus bows and leaves, two bored and idle servants, big Sampson and little Gregory, come from the Capulet house. Sampson struts about, boasting of his bravery in battle, while little Gregory teases him.)

Sampson: Gregory, I strike quickly, being moved!

Gregory: (With a chuckle) But thou art not quickly moved to strike!

Sampson: (He shouts out a challenge at the closed door of the Montague house across the square.) A dog of the house of Montague moves me!

Gregory: To move is to stir, and to be valiant is to stand. Therefore, if thou art moved, thou runnest away. *(He yawns at big Sampson's boasts.)*

Sampson: A dog of **that** house shall move me to stand! *(He growls at the Montague door again, taking a few brave steps towards it.)*

Gregory: The quarrel is between our masters and us, their men. *(The Montague door opens, and out come two similar servants, Abram and Balthasar. Sampson retreats to the Capulet doorstep, where little Gregory hides behind him and gives advice.)* Draw thy tool! Here comes two of the house of Montagues.

Sampson: (Waving his sword weakly in the face of action.) My naked weapon is out. *(He pushes the small Gregory towards the enemies.)* Quarrel! I... will back thee!

Gregory: (Trying to hide again) How? Turn thy back and run?

Sampson: (Suddenly cautious) Let us take the law of our sides. Let **them** begin. *(He puts up his sword, but he and Gregory start strolling towards the Montagues, half-afraid and half-challenging.)*

Gregory: I will frown as I pass by. *(Slowly they walk past the Montague servants, who tense and watch them.)*

Sampson: (In a whisper to Gregory.) I will bite my thumb at them, which is disgrace to them if they bear it! *(He puts his thumb in his mouth and flicks it out at the enemy servants, who quickly rise and block his path, their hands on their sword-hilts.)*

Abram: Do you bite your thumb at us, sir?

Sampson: (Innocently) I do bite my thumb, sir.

Abram: (With growing anger) Do you bite your thumb at **us**, sir?

Sampson: (Whispering to Gregory) Is the law of our side if I say, "Ay"?

Gregory: (Whispering back) No.

Sampson: (Loudly to the Montague servants.) No, sir, I do not bite my thumb at you, sir. *(The Montague*

men stand to one side with a sneer.) But I bite my thumb, sir! *(They surround him again.)*

Gregory: (Bravely trying to look taller.) Do you quarrel, sir?

Abram: Quarrel, sir? No, sir!

Sampson: (Still half-boasting) If you do, sir, I am for you! I serve as good a man as you!

Abram: No better.

Sampson: Well, sir...

Gregory: (Whispering to Sampson as he looks down the street.) Say "better." Here comes one of my master's kinsmen.

Sampson: (Stating that Capulet is better than Montague.) Yes, better, sir!

Abram: You lie! *(He and Balthasar grip their sword-hilts in quick fury.)*

Sampson: Draw, if you be men! Gregory, remember thy swashing blow! *(The four servants begin to fight with old heavy swords. Benvolio, a good-tempered young cousin of the Montagues, enters the plaza. Instantly, he tries to separate the men, beating their blades down with his slim rapier.)*

Benvolio: Part, fools! Put up your swords. You know not what you do! *(Tybalt, a Capulet cousin as sleek as a black cat, enters and draws his rapier with a smile, gliding towards Benvolio.)*

Tybalt: What, art thou drawn? Turn thee, Benvolio. Look upon thy death! *(He slices his blade through the air, making it hiss.)*

Benvolio: (Ignoring Tybalt's attack and trying to stop the servants' battle.) I do but keep the peace. Put up thy sword. Or manage it to part these men with me.

Tybalt: What, drawn, and talk of peace? I hate the word as I hate Hell, all Montagues, and thee! *(He lunges, proud of his precise swordsmanship.)* Have at thee, coward! *(Benvolio is forced to defend himself; they cross swords, and the air clangs with steel on steel.)*

(Townspeople rush in and take sides, joining the fight with cheers and noise. Some women, frightened, call for the Officer of the Law, who enters with more citizens carrying clubs and the spear-axes known as bills or partisans. They aim blows at the swords of the fighters.)

Citizens: Clubs, bills, and partisans! Strike! Beat them down. Down with the Capulets! Down with the Montagues! *(As the fight becomes a street brawl, Old Capulet appears at his doorway, gray-haired and fat, wanting to join in.)*

Capulet: What noise is this? Give me my long sword, ho!

Lady Capulet: (Unsympathetically the young wife thinks her old husband needs something else.) A crutch, a crutch! Why call you for a sword?

Capulet: My sword, I say! *(The Montague door opens and Lord Montague appears, sword in hand.)* Old Montague is come and flourishes his blade in spite of me.

Montague: Thou villain Capulet! *(As he shouts, Lady Montague clings to his arm.)* Hold me not. Let me go!

Lady Montague: Thou shalt not stir one foot to seek a foe! *(Into the riot come the Prince of Verona and his men. The courtiers help the lawmen stop the fray, as the peace-loving Prince ascends the fountain steps to address his people.)*

Prince: (In a loud voice) Rebellious subjects, enemies to peace, profaners of this neighbor-stained steel ....Will they not hear? *(He shouts angrily at the men who continue to exchange blows.)* What, ho! You men, you beasts! On pain of torture, from those bloody hands throw your mistempered weapons to the ground, and hear the sentence of your moved Prince! *(At last the rioters cease, and the courtiers bring before the Prince the leaders of the two warring houses, old Montague and Capulet. The Prince frowns at them, holding them responsible for the many recent quarrels caused by light teasing.)*

Three civil brawls, bred of an airy word by thee, old Capulet, and Montague, have thrice disturbed the quiet of our streets! *(To all)* If ever you disturb our streets again, your lives shall pay the forfeit of the peace! *(The crowd murmurs in alarm at the death penalty for future fighting, but the Prince waves to the townsfolk to be gone at once.)*

Prince: If ever you disturb our streets again, your lives shall pay the forfeit of the peace!

For this time, all the rest depart away. You, Capulet, shall go along with me. *(Old Capulet bows obediently.)* And, Montague, come you this afternoon, to know our farther pleasure in this case, to old Freetown, our common judgment place. *(Lord Montague bows as the Prince repeats his command for the crowd to disperse quietly or die.)* Once more, on pain of death, all men depart! *(He leaves with his courtiers and Old Capulet, whose broad face still looks angry. Left alone in the plaza are Lord and Lady Montague and their young nephew Benvolio, the peace-maker.)*

Montague: Who set this ancient quarrel new? Speak, nephew. Were you by when it began?

Benvolio: (Pointing about the plaza to explain the positions of the swordsmen.) Here were the servants of your adversary, and yours, close-fighting ere I did approach. I drew to part them. In the instant came the fiery Tybalt, with his sword prepared, which he swung about his head and cut the winds. While we were interchanging thrusts and blows, came more and more, and fought on part and part, till the Prince came, who parted either part.

Lady Montague: (Looking about for her young son.) O, where is Romeo? Saw you him today? Right glad I am he was not at this fray.

Benvolio: (He points in the direction of some woods outside the city, where he has seen Romeo at dawn.) Madam, an hour before the sun peered forth the golden window of the East, a troubled mind drove me to walk abroad, where, underneath the grove of sycamore that westward rooteth from the city's side, so early walking did I see your son. Towards him I made, but he was aware of me and stole into the cover of the wood.

Montague: (With wonder at his son Romeo, who wanders about weeping and sighing until daybreak, when he locks himself up in his darkened room.) Many a morning hath he there been seen, with tears augmenting the fresh morning's dew, adding to clouds more clouds with his deep sighs. But all so soon as the all-cheering sun should in the farthest East begin to draw the shady curtains from Aurora's bed, away from light steals home my heavy son, and private in his chamber pens himself, shuts up his windows, locks fair daylight out, and makes himself an artificial night.

Benvolio: (Puzzled about his cousin's strange behavior.) My noble uncle, do you know the cause?

Montague: I neither know it nor can learn of him.

Benvolio: (Curious to learn if his uncle has asked Romeo directly what is the matter.) Have you importuned him by any means?

Montague: Both by myself and many other friends. But he is to himself so secret and so close as is the bud bit with an envious worm. Could we but learn from whence his sorrows grow, we would as willingly give cure. *(He shakes his head, baffled. But Benvolio pulls his sleeve and points across the square where Romeo — young, handsome, and fashionably dressed — enters walking slowly.)*

Benvolio: See where he comes. *(He gestures towards the Montagues' front door.)* So please you, step aside. **I'll** know his grievance or be much denied!

Montague: Come, madam, let's away! *(He takes his wife's arm, and with a grateful glance at Benvolio, they go inside their house. Benvolio crosses to greet his friend and cure his mood.)*

Benvolio: Good morrow, cousin.

Romeo: (With a sigh to the heavens.) Is the day so young?

Benvolio: But new struck nine.

Romeo: Ay, me! Sad hours seem long. *(He looks at his home.)* Was that my father that went hence so fast?

Benvolio: It was. *(Romeo sits on the fountain edge, and Benvolio joins him, smiling sympathetically at his handsome cousin.)* What sadness lengthens Romeo's hours?

Romeo: Not having that which having makes them short. *(He seems to enjoy his mysterious misery.)*

Benvolio: In love?

Romeo: Out…

Benvolio: …of love?

Romeo: (Shaking his head as his sweetheart has refused to see him.) Out of her favor where I am in love.

Benvolio: (Relieved to find the trouble no worse, but still full of good-natured sympathy.) Alas!

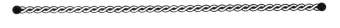

Romeo: Alas! *(His sad love-life does not keep him from eating, however.)* Where shall we dine? *(For the first time he sees the bloodstains and the traces of the battle.)* O me! What fray was here? *(He interrupts Benvolio's answer, knowing already how much the feuding families love a good fight.)* Yet tell me not, for I have heard it all. Here's much to do with hate, but more with love.

(He continues with fashionable combinations of opposite things that appear in this chaotic world.) Why, then, O brawling love! O loving hate! O anything, of nothing first create! O heavy lightness! Serious vanity! Misshapen chaos of well-seeming forms! Feather of lead, bright smoke, cold fire, sick health, still-waking sleep that is not what it is! This love feel I, that feel no love in this. *(Benvolio smiles in pity at his love-sick cousin's over-elaborate words.)* Dost thou not laugh?

Benvolio: No, coz, I rather weep.

Romeo: Good heart, at what?

Benvolio: At thy good heart's oppression.

Romeo: Griefs of mine own lie heavy in my breast. *(He sighs again, feeling the responsibility for Benvolio's brotherly affection.)* This love that thou hast shown doth add more grief to too much of mine own. *(He flings himself into poetic fancies again.)* Love is...a smoke raised with the fume of sighs. Being purged, a fire sparkling in lovers' eyes. Being vexed, a sea nourished with lovers' tears. *(He stops to make up more love-poetry.)*

What is it else? A madness most discreet, a choking gall, and a preserving sweet. *(He rises.)* Farewell, my coz.

Benvolio: (Rising to join his cousin.) Soft! I will go along. And if you leave me so, you do me wrong.

Romeo: (As he feels himself lost in love.) Tut! I have lost myself. I am not here. This is not Romeo. He's some other where.

Benvolio: (Full of curiosity to know the girl's name.) Tell me in sadness, who is that you love?

Romeo: What, shall I groan and tell thee?

Benvolio: Groan? Why, no, but sadly tell me who.

Romeo: (With great importance) In sadness, cousin, I do love…a woman.

Benvolio: (Dryly) I aimed so near when I supposed you loved.

Romeo: A right good mark-man. And she's fair I love.

Benvolio: (Talking in terms of archery, Cupid's sport.) A right fair mark, fair coz, is soonest hit.

Romeo: Well, in that hit you miss. She'll not be hit with Cupid's arrow. *(His beloved maiden has sworn to live unmarried, like the goddess Diana.)* She hath Dian's wit. From Love's weak childish bow she lives unharmed. *(He is sad that she will not pass her loveliness on to future children.)* O, she is rich in beauty; only poor that, when she dies, with beauty dies her store.

Benvolio: Then she hath sworn that she will still live chaste?

Romeo: She hath. *(The girl's decision never to love is killing him.)* She hath forsworn to love, and in that vow do I live dead that live to tell it now.

Benvolio: (With solid advice) Be ruled by me: forget to think of her!

Romeo: O, teach me how I should forget to think!

Benvolio: (Looking at some pretty girls who stroll across the plaza.) Examine other beauties.

Romeo: Tis the way to call hers exquisite. He that is strucken blind cannot forget the precious treasure of his eyesight lost. *(Sadly he looks at the girls, who only remind him of the more beautiful girl he loves.)* Show me a mistress that is "passing fair." What doth her beauty serve but as a note where I may read who passed that "passing fair"? *(He turns again to go.)* Farewell. Thou canst not teach me to forget.

Benvolio: (Willing to bet he can help.) I'll pay that doctrine, or else die in debt. *(They leave.)*

Scene 2

(In the same scene, Old Capulet returns to his house after seeing the Prince about the feud. With him is the little Count or "County" Paris, a pleasant young

relative of the Prince. Behind them walks Capulet's stupid servant, Peter. Capulet talks of the ban on fighting, and Paris nods agreement, as he hopes to marry Juliet, Capulet's daughter, soon.)

Capulet: But Montague is bound as well as I in penalty alike. And tis not hard, I think, for men so old as we to keep the peace.

Paris: (With respect for both families.) Of honorable reckoning are you both. And pity tis you lived at odds so long. *(Changing the subject, he speaks with embarrassed eagerness.)* But now, my lord, what say you to my suit?

Capulet: (Thinking Juliet is too young yet to marry.) But saying o'er what I have said before: my child is yet a stranger in the world. She hath not seen the change of fourteen years. Let two more summers wither in their pride ere we may think her ripe to be a bride.

Paris: (Arguing that it is common custom for girls to marry young.) Younger than she are happy mothers made.

Capulet: (With warning.) And too soon **marred** are those so early made! *(Unhappily he looks at a window above, where his pretty young wife is laughing with their handsome young cousin Tybalt. But his attention turns again to Juliet, his only surviving child.)* The earth hath swallowed all my hopes but she. She is the hopeful lady of my earth. *(With friendliness)* But woo her, gentle Paris. Get her heart. *(He will let Juliet help decide.)* My will to her consent is but a part.

(He takes his arm in confidence.) This night I hold an old-accustomed feast whereto I have invited many a guest, such as I love. And you, among the store, one more, most welcome, makes my number more. *(Paris smiles at the chance to finally meet Juliet at the party. Capulet opens the door to his house.)* Come, go with me.

(As he enters, he turns and gives Peter a guest list.) Go, sirrah, trudge about through fair Verona. Find those persons out whose names are written there. And to them say, my house and welcome on their pleasure stay. *(He and Paris go in, leaving Peter to stare stupidly at the list. He turns it upside-down and rightside-up, scratching his head. He cannot read.)*

Peter: Find them out whose names are written here? I am sent to find those persons whose names are here writ, and can never find what names the writing person hath here writ. I must to the learned! *(He spies Romeo and Benvolio approach. Since they are gentlemen, they will know how to read, and he steps into their path to get their attention.)* In good time!

Benvolio: (To Romeo, still trying to cure one love by finding another.) Tut, man, one fire burns out another's burning. Take thou some new infection to thy eye, and the rank poison of the old will die.

Romeo: (Quoting a household remedy for scratches.) Your plantain leaf is excellent for that.

Benvolio: (Not understanding that Romeo is teasing him.) Why, Romeo, art thou mad?

Romeo: (Reciting his lover's tortures) Not mad, but
bound more than a madman is, shut up in prison,
kept without my food, whipped and tormented
and.... *(He bumps into Peter, who waves the paper
in his face.)* God-den, good fellow.

Peter: (Returning the "Good-evening" greeting.) God
gi' go-den. I pray, sir, can you read?

Romeo: (Teasing) Ay, mine own fortune in my misery.

Peter: But, I pray, can you read anything you see?

Romeo: Ay, if I know the letters and the language.

*Peter: (Puzzled, he decides to leave and try someone
else.)* Ye say honestly. Rest you merry. *(He starts
to go, but Romeo stops him and takes the paper
with kindness.)*

Romeo: Stay, fellow. I can read. *(He glances at the list
of names.)* "Signior Martino and his wife and
daughters. County Anselmo and his beauteous
sisters. *(Benvolio whistles appreciatively and
rolls his eyes.)* The lady widow of Vitruvio. *(Both
Romeo and Benvolio make sour faces.)* Signior
Placentio and his lovely nieces. Mercutio and his
brother Valentine. *(Romeo and Benvolio become
interested, as Mercutio is their best friend.)* Mine
uncle Capulet, his wife and daughters. My fair
niece Rosaline!

*(The young men grow excited, as Rosaline is
Romeo's hopeless love. He hurries through the rest
of the names.)* And Livia, Signior Valentio and his
cousin Tybalt; Lucio and the lively Helena."
(Peter, meanwhile, has counted the names off on

his fingers, memorizing them. Romeo returns the paper to him.) A fair assembly. Whither should they come?

Peter: Up.

Romeo: Whither?

Peter: (Smiling stupidly) To supper. To our house.

Romeo: Whose house?

Peter: My master's!

Romeo: Indeed, I should have asked you that before. *(He and Benvolio laugh.)*

Peter: Now I'll tell you without asking. My master is the great rich Capulet. And if you be not of the house of Montagues, I pray come and crush a cup of wine! *(He bows to them as he leaves.)* Rest you merry!

Benvolio: (Delighted at the opportunity for Romeo to compare his love with even prettier girls.) At this same ancient feast of Capulet's sups the fair Rosaline, whom thou so lovest, with all the admired beauties of Verona. Go thither, and compare her face with some that I shall show. And I will make thee think thy "swan" a crow!

Romeo: One fairer than my love? *(He laughs)* The all-seeing sun ne'er saw her match since first the world begun.

Benvolio: Tut! You saw her fair, none else being by. Let there be weighed your lady-love against some other maid that I will show you shining at this feast.

Romeo: (Refusing to think anyone could be more beautiful than his Rosaline.) I'll go along, no such sight to be shown, but to rejoice in splendor of mine own. *(In good spirits, they leave to prepare to secretly attend the feast of the enemy family.)*

Scene 3

(In Capulet's house, young Lady Capulet speaks to Juliet's jolly fat old Nurse, who loves long stories of the past and earthy peasant jokes about marriage and sex. Lady Capulet, already dressed for the festivities, seems impatient as she sits, waiting.)

Lady Capulet: Nurse, where's my daughter? Call her forth to me.

Nurse: (With rough good humor) Now, by my maidenhead at twelve year old, I bade her come. *(Calls loudly)* What, lamb! What, ladybird! *(To herself, slightly cross.)* God forbid, where's this girl? *(Calls again)* What, **Juliet!**

Juliet: (Entering rather slowly, a lovely girl of thirteen, wearing an elaborate white gown for the gala.) How now? Who calls?

Nurse: Your mother!

Juliet: (Instantly obedient, she goes to her mother and kneels with formal greeting.) Madam, I am here. What is your will?

Lady Capulet: This is the matter....*(She looks at the Nurse, who is obviously listening.)* Nurse, give leave awhile. We must talk in secret. *(The Nurse, making a sour face, starts to go, but Lady Capulet changes her mind.)* Nurse, come back again. I have remembered me...thou's hear our counsel. *(The Nurse returns, all smiles, as Lady Capulet speaks to her.)* Thou knowest my daughter's of a pretty age. *(She motions to Juliet to sit on a footstool.)*

Nurse: Faith, I can tell her age unto an hour.

Lady Capulet: She's not fourteen.

Nurse: (Smiling toothlessly) I'll lay fourteen of my teeth — and yet, to my teen be it spoken, I have but four — she's not fourteen. How long is it now to Lammastide?

Lady Capulet: (Counting two weeks and more.) A fortnight and odd days.

Nurse: Even or odd, of all days in the year, come Lammas Eve at night shall she be fourteen. Susan and she — God rest all Christian souls! — were of an age. Well, Susan is with God. *(She makes a pious Sign of the Cross in memory of her dead child.)* She was too good for me. But, as I said, on Lammas Eve at night shall she be fourteen. That shall she, marry! *(She nods her head.)* I remember it well. Tis since the earthquake now eleven years. And she was weaned — I never shall forget it — of all the days of the year, upon that day. For I had then laid wormwood to my dug, sitting in the sun under the dove-house wall. My lord and you were then at Mantua. *(She taps her head shrewdly, proud of her excellent memory for details, and both Juliet and her mother sigh at the Nurse's long-windedness.)* Nay, I do bear a brain! And since that time it is eleven years. For then she could stand high-lone...Nay, by the rood, she could have run and waddled all about!

(She recalls Juliet's bumping her head.) For even the day before, she broke her brow. And then my husband — God be with his soul! He was a merry man — took up the child. "Yea," quoth he, "dost thou fall upon thy face? Thou wilt fall backward when thou hast more wit, wilt thou not, Jule?" And, by my holidame, the pretty wretch left crying and said, "Ay." *(She laughs heartily at the child's being tricked into agreeing with such a naughty remark.)* And I should live a thousand years, I never should forget it. "Wilt thou not, Jule?" quoth he, and, pretty fool, it stinted and said, "Ay."

Lady Capulet: Enough of this. I pray thee, hold thy peace!

Nurse: (Not aware she is boring them, she starts to repeat the story all over.) Yes, madam. Yet I cannot choose but laugh to think it should leave crying and say, "Ay." And yet, I warrant, it had upon it brow a bump as big as a young cockrel's stone. A perilous knock! And it cried bitterly. "Yea," quoth my husband, "fallest upon thy face? Thou wilt fall backward when thou comest to age, wilt thou not, Jule?" It stinted and said, "Ay." *(The Nurse wipes tears of laughter from her face.)*

Juliet: And stint thou too, I pray thee, Nurse, say I.

Nurse: Peace, I have done. *(She kisses Juliet fondly.)*
God mark thee to His grace! Thou wast the
prettiest babe that e'er I nursed. And I might live
to see thee married once, I have my wish.

Lady Capulet: (Firmly taking over the conversation.)
Marry, that "marry" is the very theme I came to
talk of. Tell me, daughter Juliet, how stands your
disposition to be married?

Juliet: (Shyly) It is an honor that I dream not of.

Nurse: An honor? *(She smiles with approval.)*

Lady Capulet: (Raising her daughter to sit beside her.)
Well, think of marriage now. Younger than you,
here in Verona, ladies of esteem, are made already
mothers. *(She adjusts her festive headdress
prettily.)* By my count, I was your mother much
upon these years that you are now a maid. Thus,
then in brief: the valiant Paris seeks you for his
love!

*Nurse: (Throwing up her hands in admiration of the
count, who is as perfect as a statue.)* A man, young
lady! Lady, such a man as all the world…Why,
he's a man of wax!

Lady Capulet: (Agreeing) Verona's summer hath not
such a flower.

Nurse: Nay, he's a flower, in faith…a very flower!

Lady Capulet: (To Juliet) What say you? Can you love
the gentleman? *(Juliet looks at the floor and
shrugs.)* This night you shall behold him at our

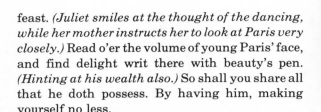

feast. *(Juliet smiles at the thought of the dancing, while her mother instructs her to look at Paris very closely.)* Read o'er the volume of young Paris' face, and find delight writ there with beauty's pen. *(Hinting at his wealth also.)* So shall you share all that he doth possess. By having him, making yourself no less.

Nurse: No less? Nay, **bigger!** *(She sees Juliet married and the first baby on the way already.)* Women grow by men!

Lady Capulet: (To her daughter) Speak briefly, can you like of Paris' love?

Juliet: (Obediently willing to try) I'll look to like, if looking liking move. *(But she will await her parent's approval.)* But no more deep will I endart mine eye than your consent gives strength to make it fly. *(They are interrupted by Peter, who stumbles in, confused with preparations for the feast.)*

Peter: Madam, the guests are come, supper served up, you called, my young lady asked for, the Nurse cursed in the pantry, and everything in extremity! I must hence. I beseech you, follow straight! *(He rushes out.)*

Lady Capulet: We follow thee! *(To Juliet, whose young count is waiting.)* Juliet, the County stays.

Nurse: (Excited at the coming marriage.) Go, girl, seek happy nights to happy days. *(She pushes Juliet out the door with her youthful mother, both looking forward to the festivities.)*

Scene 4

(In the plaza, torches light the darkness before the Capulet house. Romeo and Benvolio have been joined by their quicksilver friend, Mercutio, always eager for a joke or trick, and several other young masked friends. They are disguised, following the custom for young men-about-town to invade a fashionable party, give a speech of apology and dance with all the ladies. Hosts always welcomed them, for they livened up a feast. Romeo waves a scroll at the others.)

Romeo: (What, shall this speech be spoke for our excuse? Or shall we on without apology?

Benvolio: (Only wanting to dance a little.) We'll measure them a measure and be gone.

Romeo: (Putting away the speech, he takes the torch from Mercutio.) Give me a torch. I am not for this ambling. *(He gives a love-lorn sigh.)* Being but heavy, I will bear the light.

Mercutio: Nay, gentle Romeo, we must have you dance. *(He starts practicing dance steps.)*

Romeo: Not I, believe me. You have dancing shoes with nimble soles. I have a soul of lead.

Mercutio: You are a lover. Borrow Cupid's wings!

Romeo: Under love's heavy burden do I sink. Is love a tender thing? It is too rough, too rude, too boisterous, and it pricks like thorn.

Mercutio: If love be rough with you, be rough with love! *(He calls for a mask to cover his funny ugly face.)* Give me a case to put my visage in. A visor for a visor! *(Benvolio hands out some masks, and they approach Capulet's door.)*

Benvolio: Come, knock and enter! *(He does a little fancy dance step.)* And no sooner in, but every man betake him to his legs.

Romeo: A torch for me! I'll be a candleholder and look on.

Mercutio: (Eager not to waste time.) Come, we burn daylight, ho!

Romeo: (Lagging behind) And we mean well in going to this masque. But tis no wit to go.

Mercutio: Why, may one ask?

Romeo: (Thinking of last night's bad dream, with a sense of horror.) I dreamt a dream tonight.

Mercutio: And so did I!

Romeo: (Smiling in spite of himself.) Well, what was yours?

Mercutio: That dreamers often lie...

Romeo: ...in bed asleep, while they do dream things true.

Mercutio: (For fun, he clowns about, describing Queen Mab, the dream-fairy, small as the agate stone in the ring of a city elder. She drives a little chariot with wheel-spokes of spider legs and other oddments including a driver who is a gnat.)

O, then I see Queen Mab hath been with you! She is the fairies' midwife. And she comes in shape no bigger than an agate stone on the forefinger of an alderman, drawn with a team of little atomies athwart men's noses as they lie asleep. Her wagon spokes made of long spinners' legs; the cover, of the wings of grasshoppers; her traces, of the smallest spider's web; her collars, of the moon-shine's watery beams; her whip of cricket's bone; the lash of film; her wagoner, a small gray-coated gnat not half so big as a round little worm pricked from the lazy finger of a maid. Her chariot is an empty hazel-nut made by the joiner squirrel or old grub, time out of mind the fairies' coach-makers. And in this state she gallops night by night through lovers' brains, and then they dream of love....

Romeo: Peace, peace, Mercutio, peace! Thou talkest of nothing!

Mercutio: (Rattling on happily, trying to make Romeo smile.) True, I talk of dreams, which are the children of an idle brain, begot of nothing but vain fantasy, which is as thin of substance as the air and more inconstant than the wind.

Benvolio: (Eager to go on to the party.) This wind you talk of blows us from ourselves. Supper is done, and we shall come too late.

Romeo: (With a sudden shiver) I fear too early! *(The others stop, surprised at his hollow voice. He explains, puzzled, that he feels something tragic, some future fate will begin at this same feast and end in death.)* For my mind misgives — some consequence yet hanging in the stars shall bitterly

begin his fearful date with this night's revels...
and expire the term of a despised life by untimely
death. *(The others, chilled to the bone by this
prophecy, cross themselves. But Romeo tries to
cheer them by saying his life is still in God's
hands.)* But He that hath the steerage of my
course, direct my sail! On, lusty gentlemen!
*(Recovering their spirits, they go to the Capulet's
door. Romeo puts on his mask also.)*

Benvolio: (Knocking) Strike, drum!

Scene 5

*(As the action continues, the door opens and they enter
the house, where the servants are scurrying about,
clearing plates and pushing back the furniture to
make room for dancing.)*

1st Servingman: Where's Potpan, that he helps not to
take away? *(He waves a napkin at the others.)*
Away with the join-stools, remove the court-
cupboard, look to the plate! *(To a servant
removing a dish of candy.)* Good thou, save me a
piece of marchpane! *(He calls two others to come
help.)* Anthony and Potpan!

2nd Servingman: Ay, boy, ready.

1st Servingman: (Angrily) You are looked for and
called for, asked for and sought for, in the great
chamber!

3rd Servingman: We cannot be here and there too. *(He helps the others move the furniture back.)* Cheerly, boys! Be brisk awhile! *(As the servants busy themselves, Capulet, his wife, Juliet, Tybalt, Nurse and guests enter to dance. They welcome the maskers happily, knowing they will dance and flirt and be merry.)*

Capulet: (Going forward to shake the maskers' hands.) Welcome, gentlemen! *(He laughs to the guests.)* Ladies that have their toes un-plagued with corns will have a bout with you! *(He teases the women.)* Ah ha, my mistresses, which of you all will now deny to dance? She that makes dainty...she, I'll swear, hath corns! *(To the maskers, recalling his own masking days of youth.)* Welcome, gentlemen! I have seen the day that I have worn a visor and could tell a whispering tale in a fair lady's ear, such as would please! *(He shakes his old head and laughs.)* Tis gone...tis gone...tis gone! *(He leads them to the dance floor.)* You are welcome, gentlemen! Come, musicians, play!

(A small band of musicians strike up a lively dance, all the maskers but Romeo choose partners, and other couples join them. Capulet, a jolly host, goes about, making some stand back and others dance, giving orders to the servants also.) A hall, a hall! Give room! And foot it, girls! More light, you knaves, and turn the tables up. And quench the fire — the room is grown too hot. *(He speaks to Romeo, the only masker not dancing.)* Ah, sirrah, this unlooked-for sport comes well! *(He helps an elderly relative to a bench to sit and watch.)* Nay,

sit. Nay, sit, good cousin Capulet. For you and I
are past our dancing days. How long is it now
since last yourself and I were in a mask?

Old Man: By Our Lady, thirty years.

Capulet: What, man? Tis not so much, tis not so much!

Old Man: Tis more, tis more! *(They watch the dancers
with smiles on their old faces.)*

*(Romeo at first gazes on the scene with mild
interest, his eyes searching only for his lady-love,
the cold-hearted Rosaline. But Juliet dances by
with Paris, and Romeo is thunder-struck. In one
glance, she has taken his heart. He puts his torch-
light into a wall sconce and starts to follow her,
keeping safely in the shadows while he takes off
his mask. As a servingman passes, Romeo touches
his sleeve and speaks.)*

Romeo: (Pointing to Juliet) What lady's that which
doth enrich the hand of yonder knight?

Servingman: I know not, sir. *(He leaves.)*

*Romeo: (As he watches Juliet's bright face and white
dress against the shadows of the torchlit hall, he
whispers to his beating heart.)* O, she doth teach
the torches to burn bright! It seems she hangs
upon the cheek of night like a rich jewel in an
Ethiop's ear — beauty too rich for use, for earth too
dear! So shows a snowy dove trooping with crows,
as yonder lady o'er her fellows shows. *(He vows to
meet her after the dance is over, to worship her as a
saint.)* The measure done, I'll watch her place of
stand and, touching hers, make blessed my rude
hand!

Romeo: O, she doth teach the torches to burn bright!

(His former love, dark Rosaline, dances past, and Romeo masks his face from her.) Did my heart love till now? Forswear it, sight! For I ne'er saw true beauty till this night! *(Eagerly he looks again at Juliet. But Romeo's voice has caught the ear of Juliet's sharp-tempered cousin Tybalt, who is passing.)*

Tybalt: (To himself) This, by his voice, should be a Montague. *(To a nearby servant)* Fetch me my rapier, boy! *(He is furious, thinking Romeo comes to laugh at their feast from behind his mask.)* What! Dares the slave come hither, covered with an antic face, to scorn at our solemnity? Now, by the stock and honor of my kin, to strike him dead I hold it not a sin!

Capulet: (Catching sight of Tybalt's frown.) Why, how now, kinsman? Wherefore storm you so?

Tybalt: (Pointing to Romeo, who still gazes spellbound at Juliet.) Uncle, this is a Montague, our foe! A villain that is hither come in spite to scorn at our solemnity this night.

Capulet: (Peering through the gloom, he sees Romeo lower his mask again.) Young Romeo, is it?

Tybalt: Tis he, that villain Romeo!

Capulet: (Quietly) Content thee, gentle coz. Let him alone. He bears him like a portly gentleman. And, to say truth, Verona brags of him to be a virtuous and well-governed youth. Therefore be patient — take no note of him. *(Tybalt continues to look*

angry, and Capulet begins to lose his temper.) It is my will! Show a fair presence and put off these frowns!

Tybalt: It fits when such a villain is a guest! *(In a cold fury)* I'll not endure him!

Capulet: (Totally enraged that young Tybalt should disregard his peace-making and want to turn the party into a brawl.) He **shall** be endured! What, goodman boy! **I** say he shall! Go to! Am I the master here, or you? Go to! **You'll** not endure him? **You'll** make mutiny among my guests? **You** will set cock-a-hoop? **You'll** be the man? *(He gives a loud snort of scorn.)*

Tybalt: (Pleading) Why, uncle, tis a shame!

Capulet: (Furious with Tybalt, whom he scolds, still he tries to appear the jolly host to the guests as the dancing stops.) Go to, go to! You are a saucy boy! *(To the guests)* Well said, my hearts! *(To Tybalt)* You are a princox — go! Be quiet, or.... *(To the servants)* More light, more light! *(To Tybalt)* For shame! I'll make you quiet. What! *(To the guests)* Cheerly, my hearts! *(With a last scowl at Tybalt, he joins his guests in drinking.)*

Tybalt: (To himself, angrily) I will withdraw, But this intrusion shall, now seeming sweet, convert to bitterest gall. *(He goes off, vowing to have revenge.)*

(As the dance ends, Juliet turns and come face-to-face with Romeo, who looks deeply into her eyes as he takes her hand. She looks at him as if in a

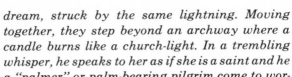

dream, struck by the same lightning. Moving together, they step beyond an archway where a candle burns like a church-light. In a trembling whisper, he speaks to her as if she is a saint and he a "palmer" or palm-bearing pilgrim come to worship the shrine of her hand, which he holds reverently in his.)

Romeo: If I profane with my unworthiest hand this holy shrine, the gentle fine is this: my lips, two blushing pilgrims, ready stand, to smooth that rough touch with a tender kiss. *(He kisses the palm of her hand, as if kissing away the "sin" of his touch.)*

(Magnetized, she continues the poem he has begun, and in the pretended worship, she encourages his "good manners.")

Juliet: Good Pilgrim, you do wrong your hand too much, which mannerly devotion shows in this. For saints have hands that pilgrims' hands do touch...*(She slides her hand into his.)*...and palm-to-palm is holy palmer's kiss!

Romeo: (Coming closer) Have not saints lips, and holy palmers too? *(He bends to kiss her mouth, but she moves back a little, with a half-teasing smile.)*

Juliet: Ay, Pilgrim, lips that they must use in prayer.

Romeo: (Looking at their joined hands.) O, then, dear Saint, let lips do what hands do! **They** pray. *(Again he bends to kiss her.)* Grant thou, lest faith turn to despair....

Juliet: (In an attempt to look cold and saintly.) Saints do not move...*(She breaks into a sudden smile, though, for saints do answer prayers.)*...though grant, for prayers' sake!

Romeo: (As his lips come near to hers, he prays for a kiss ardently.) Then move not, while my prayer's effect I take! *(Their lips meet gently.)* Thus from my lips, by yours, my "sin" is purged!

Juliet: (In mock dismay) Then have my lips the "sin" that they have took!

Romeo: "Sin" from my lips? O trespass sweetly urged! Give me my "sin" again. *(He kisses her a second time, more eagerly.)*

Juliet: (Swearing on the Bible he kisses well.) You kiss, by the Book! *(They are about to embrace a third time when the Nurse comes bustling over to chaperone. The lovers move apart, and Romeo replaces his mask.)*

Nurse: (To Juliet) Madam, your mother craves a word with you! *(Juliet formally curtsies to Romeo, who bows as she leaves. She goes only a few steps before she turns to look at him again. They stand for a moment, dazed with love and wonder. Then quickly she is gone. The Nurse is about to follow when Romeo catches her sleeve, hoping to find out the name of Juliet's family.)*

Romeo: What is her mother?

Nurse: (Happy and boasting) Marry, bachelor, her mother is the lady of the house, and a good lady, and a wise and virtuous. I nursed her daughter that you talked withal. *(Confidentially, she lets him know of Juliet's rich dowry.)* I tell you, he that can lay hold of her shall have "the chinks." *(She tosses imaginary coins in the air as she goes to join Juliet. Romeo is left stunned at his new love's identity.)*

Romeo: Is she a Capulet? O dear account! My life is my foe's debt!

Benvolio: (Coming to take Romeo away, leaving the party a success.) Away, be gone! The sport is at the best.

Romeo: (Bewildered by the events) Ay, so I fear. The more is my unrest.

Capulet: (Urging them to stay for a midnight supper.) Nay, gentlemen, prepare not to be gone! We have a trifling foolish banquet towards. *(But Benvolio, Mercutio and Romeo bow and go to the door, shaking his hands in thanks for the hospitality.)* Is it even so? Why then, I thank you all. *(The other guests also prepare to leave. Capulet bids them goodbye.)* I thank you, honest gentlemen! Good night....*(To the servants)* More torches here! *(As the last go, Capulet speaks to his wife.)* Come on then. Let's to bed. *(Yawning happily, he and his wife leave. Juliet stays watching the departing guests out of sight. Her eyes search for Romeo, and she calls the Nurse to help her, as she pretends to be interested in all the young men.)*

Juliet: Come hither, Nurse. What is yond gentleman?

Nurse: The son and heir of old Tiberio.

Juliet: What's he that now is going out of door?

Nurse: Marry, that, I think be young Petruchio.

Juliet: (Pointing out Romeo) What's he that follows there, that would not dance?

Nurse: I know not.

Juliet: Go ask his name. *(As the Nurse hurries after Romeo, Juliet has a horrifying thought.)* If he be married, my grave is like to be my wedding bed!

Nurse: (Returning with a serious face.) His name is Romeo, and a Montague, the only son of your great enemy!

Juliet: (To herself, in shock, realizing she has fallen in love with the wrong person.) My only love, sprung from my only hate! Too early seen unknown, and known too late! *(She feels such love is basically wrong, confused, chaotic.)* Prodigious birth of love it is to me, that I must love a loathed enemy.

Nurse: (Half-hearing her speak) What's this? What's this?

Juliet: (Making up an excuse) A rhyme I learnt even now of one I danced withal. *(From the inner house comes a call, "Juliet!")*

Nurse: (In response that she will come at once.) Anon, anon! *(To Juliet)* Come, let's away, The strangers all are gone. *(As they leave, Juliet pauses to look back at the archway where she and Romeo kissed.)*

ACT II

Scene 1

(In the dark plaza outside the Capulet house, guests depart, guarded by servants carrying torches. Romeo appears, holding his torch and wearing his mask. But his steps lag. He looks backwards at the house.)

Romeo: (To himself) Can I go forward when my heart is here? Turn back, dull earth, and find thy center out! *(Throwing down his mask and his torch at the foot of the wall surrounding the Capulet garden, he climbs up a vine and disappears over the top of the wall as Benvolio and Mercutio appear with the last of the guests leaving the feast. The young men call out.)*

Benvolio: Romeo! My cousin Romeo! Ro—me—o!

Mercutio: (Yawning) He is wise and, on my life, hath stolen him home to bed.

Benvolio: (Catching sight of the mask and torch, which is flickering out.) He ran this way and leaped this orchard wall! Call, good Mercutio!

Mercutio: (His sense of fun returns.) Nay, I'll conjure too! *(He leaps up the steps to the fountain and makes great gestures like a magician raising spirits.)* Romeo! Humors! Madman! Passion! Lover! Appear thou in the likeness of a sigh! Speak

but one rhyme and I am satisfied! *(He makes dramatic movements.)* Cry but, "Ay, me!" Pronounce but "love" and "dove"!

(He seems overcome by his failure to make Romeo appear in a puff of smoke.) He heareth not, he stirreth not, he moveth not. The ape is **dead!** *(Solemnly)* And I must conjure him.

(He throws back his cloak and waves his sword like a magician's wand as he uses Romeo's lady-love as a magic charm to make him appear.) I conjure thee by Rosaline's bright eyes, by her high forehead and her scarlet lip...*(He looks about, but no Romeo comes, so Mercutio goes on trying to raise him.)*...by her fine foot, straight leg and quivering thigh, and the demesnes that there adjacent lie...*(He pretends to be shocked at his own suggestive words.)*...that in thy likeness thou appear to us! *(No one comes. In defeat, Mercutio "dies" elaborately down the fountain steps. Benvolio applauds and tries to pick him up off the ground.)*

Benvolio: And if he hear thee, thou wilt anger him.

Mercutio: (Feebly) This cannot anger him. *(He flaps a "dying" hand)* In his mistress' name, I conjure only but to raise up him!

Benvolio: (Letting Mercutio drop with a thump on the ground.) Come, he hath hid himself among these trees. Blind is his love and best befits the dark.

Mercutio: If love be blind, love cannot hit the mark. *(Calls out)* Romeo, good night! *(Yawns and slowly*

rises) I'll to my truckle bed. This field-bed is too
cold for me to sleep. Come, shall we go?

Benvolio: Go then. *(Singing loudly, they make their
ways home.)*

Scene 2

*(On the other side of the wall, in the Capulet orchard,
Romeo listens to Mercutio's clowning and smiles. He
knows his friends have never been wounded by
Cupid's arrows.)*

Romeo: He jests at scars that never felt a wound.
*(Above, Juliet appears at a balcony window that
overlooks the garden. She leans on the balcony
railing, gazing at the moon, which she seems to
outshine in her white dress. Romeo moves towards
her, speaking only to himself.)* But soft, what light
through yonder window breaks? It is the East, and
Juliet is the sun! Arise, fair sun, and kill the
envious moon, who is already sick and pale with
grief that thou, her maid, art far more fair than
she. It is my lady! O, it is my love! O, that she
knew she were!

(Juliet murmurs something to herself.) She
speaks, yet she says nothing. What of that? *(He
feels that even her eyes are speaking.)* Her eye
discourses. I will answer it. *(He starts forward but
backs away uncertainly.)* I am too bold. Tis not to
me she speaks.

(Juliet rests her face softly on her hand.) See how she leans her cheek upon her hand! O, that I were a glove upon that hand, that I might touch that cheek!

Juliet: (Sighing) Ay, me....

Romeo: (To himself still) She speaks! *(Above in the moonlight, she looks even more like a heavenly spirit.)* O speak again, Bright Angel, for thou art as glorious to this night, being o'er my head, as is a winged messenger of Heaven!

Juliet: (Murmuring) O Romeo, Romeo! *(Full of love, she cannot understand why he should be an enemy to her house.)* Wherefore art thou "Romeo"? *(Either he should leave his family or she should reject hers.)* Deny thy father, and refuse thy name! Or... if thou wilt not, be but sworn my love, and I'll no longer be a Capulet!

Romeo: (To himself, overjoyed) Shall I hear more, or shall I speak at this?

Juliet: (Still dreaming aloud) Tis but thy **name** that is my enemy. Thou art...thyself! What's "Montague"? It is nor hand, nor foot, nor arm, nor face, nor any other part belonging to a man. O, be some other name! What's in a name? That which we call a "rose" by any other name would smell as sweet. So Romeo would, were he not "Romeo" called, retain that dear perfection which he owns without that title. *(If he puts away his name, in return she will be his love.)* Romeo, doff thy name! And for that name, which is no part of thee, take all myself!

Romeo: (Emerging from the shadows and standing below her balcony, he calls out happily.) I take thee at thy word! Call me but "Love," and I'll be new-baptized! Henceforth, I never will be "Romeo"!

Juliet: (Startled at the unexpected man below her.) What man art thou, that, thus bescreened in night, so stumblest on my counsel?

Romeo: By a **name** I know not how to tell thee who I am. My name, dear Saint, is hateful to myself because it is an enemy to thee.

Juliet: (From the key-word "Saint" of the love-game played at the dance, and the sound of his voice, she recognizes him. Her face glows with joy as she bends over the railing of the balcony to talk.) My ears have not yet drunk a hundred words of thy tongue's utterance, yet I know the sound! Art thou not Romeo? *(Pausing)* And a Montague?

Romeo: (With a laugh) Neither, fair maid, if either thee dislike.

Juliet: (Bewildered that he could appear within the orchard.) How camest thou hither, tell me, and wherefore? The orchard walls are high and hard to climb! *(Her voice sinks to a whisper.)* And the place death, considering who thou art, if any of my kinsmen find thee here!

Romeo: (To her realistic questions he gives poetic answers.) With Love's light wings did I o'erperch these walls. For stony limits cannot hold love out. Therefore thy kinsmen are no let to me.

Juliet: If they do see thee, they will murder thee!

Romeo: (Feeling much more likely to die of love-sickness than swordplay.) Alack, there lies more peril in thine eye than twenty of their swords.

Juliet: (With admiration for his bravery) I would not for the world they saw thee here!

Romeo: I have night's cloak to hide me from their sight. *(As they smile, the thought of danger slips away in the happiness of being together.)*

Juliet: By whose direction foundest thou out this place?

Romeo: (Putting the blame on blind Cupid.) By Love, who first did prompt me to inquire. He lent me counsel, and I lent him eyes. *(He would go to the ends of the world for her.)* I am no pilot; yet, wert thou as far as that vast shore washed with the farthest sea, I would adventure for such merchandise!

Juliet: (Blushing that he has overheard her declaration of love for him.) Thou knowest the mask of night is on my face. Else would a maiden blush bepaint my cheek for that which thou hast heard me speak tonight. *(She would rather have a formal courtship, pretending she has said nothing, but it is too late.)* Fain would I dwell on form...fain, fain deny what I have spoke. But, farewell, compliment! *(She clasps her hands with seriousness, all traces of flirtation gone.)* Dost thou love me? I know thou wilt say, "Ay," and I will take thy word. O gentle Romeo, if thou dost love, pronounce it faithfully!

*(A worry rises, that he would rather have her flirt
with him.)* Or, if thou thinkest I am too quickly
won, I'll frown and be perverse and say thee,
"Nay," so thou wilt woo...but else, not for the
world!

*(Her sudden love may make him think her easily
won by any man.)* In truth, fair Montague, I am
too fond. And therefore thou mayst think my
behavior "light." But trust me, gentleman, I'll
prove more true than those that have more
cunning to be strange. *(She would have pretended
to be distant, except he overheard her admit her
love to herself.)* I should have been more strange, I
must confess, but that thou overheardst, ere I was
aware, my true-love's passion. Therefore, pardon
me, and not impute this yielding to "light" love
which the dark night hath so discovered!

Romeo: *(Starting to swear his love on romantic objects
like the moon.)* Lady, by yonder blessed moon I
swear, that tips with silver all these fruit-tree
tops...

Juliet: *(Interrupting)* O swear not by the moon, the
inconstant moon, that monthly changes in her
circled orb, lest that thy love prove likewise
variable!

Romeo: What shall I swear by?

Juliet: Do not swear at all. *(Her voice grows warm.)* Or
if thou wilt, swear by thy gracious self, which is
the god of my idolatry, and I'll believe thee!

Romeo: If my heart's dear love...

Juliet: (Interrupting again, this time uneasily.) Well, do not swear. *(She rises with the feeling that their love has happened much too fast.)* Although I joy in thee, I have no joy of this contract tonight. It is too rash, too unadvised, too sudden...too like the lightning, which doth cease to be, ere one can say, "It lightens!"

(She blows him a kiss, hoping their love will grow and bloom even more with time.) Sweet, good night. This bud of love, by summer's ripening breath, may prove a beauteous flower when next we meet. *(She starts to leave.)* Good night, good night. *(With the hope he is as happy as she.)* As sweet repose and rest come to thy heart as that within my breast!

Romeo: O, wilt thou leave me so unsatisfied?

Juliet: (Returning a little, curious) What satisfaction canst thou have tonight?

Romeo: The exchange of thy love's faithful vow for mine.

Juliet: (Simply) I gave thee mine before thou didst request it. *(She smiles, teasing him by hinting she wants her love back.)* And yet I would it were to give again.

Romeo: Wouldst thou withdraw it? For what purpose, love?

Juliet: But to be frank and give it thee again. And yet I wish but for the thing I have. *(Her love makes her generous.)* My bounty is as boundless as the sea, my love as deep. The more I give to thee, the more I have, for both are infinite. *(A sound in her bed-*

chamber makes her turn.) I hear some noise within. Dear love, adieu! *(The Nurse calls from inside the room, "Juliet! Juliet!" and she answers she will come immediately.)* Anon, good Nurse! *(To Romeo)* Sweet Montague, be true. Stay but a little. I will come again! *(She leaves the balcony. Romeo, below, looks upward at the stars, wondering if he is dreaming.)*

Romeo: O blessed, blessed night! I am afeard, being in night, all this is but a dream, too flattering-sweet to be substantial. *(Juliet appears at her balcony window again. Romeo climbs up, by vines and carvings in the stone, and clings to the edge of the balcony. She leans over and they kiss, at first almost childishly and then with hungry passion.)*

Juliet: *(Referring to the three words "I love you.")* Three words, dear Romeo and good night indeed. *(The kiss has left her so shaken that she proposes to him.)* If that thy bent of love be honorable, thy purpose marriage, send me word tomorrow by one that I'll procure to come to thee, where and what time thou wilt perform the rite. And all my fortunes at thy foot I'll lay, and follow thee, my lord, throughout the world.

(The Nurse calls again, "Madam!" and Juliet responds quickly.) I come anon! *(To Romeo, continuing her speech of love.)* But if thou meanest not well, I do beseech thee...

(The Nurse calls sharply, "Madam!" and Juliet answers with impatience.) By and by I come! *(She*

asks Romeo that, if he does not want to marry her, he stop the attack on her heart.)...to cease thy strife and leave me to my grief.

(He kisses her again with reassurance, and for a moment they cling together. Then, gently she pushes him away.) Tomorrow will I send.

Romeo: So thrive my soul....*(He descends and stands upon the ground.)*

Juliet: A thousand times good night! *(She darts into the house to quiet the Nurse.)*

Romeo: (The light of his life has gone.) A thousand times the worse, to want thy light! *(With a rueful smile, he thinks how different love and school-work seem.)* Love goes toward love as schoolboys from their books. But love from love, toward school with heavy looks. *(He turns to leave.)*

Juliet: (Returning to her balcony window, she gives a falconer's whistle as if Romeo were a pet bird.) Hist! Romeo, hist! O for a falconer's voice to lure this tassel-gentle back again! *(He steps into the moonlight once more and she sees that he did not go.)* My Romeo! *(Her face is radiant.)*

Romeo: (With equal ecstasy) It is my soul that calls upon my name! How silver-sweet sound lovers' tongues by night, like softest music to attending ears!

Juliet: Romeo....

Romeo: My sweet?

Juliet: At what o'clock tomorrow shall I send to thee?

Romeo: At the hour of nine.

Juliet: I will not fail. Tis twenty years till then. *(A happy pause rises between them. It lasts so long that Juliet laughs from embarrassment.)* I have forgot why I did call thee back.

Romeo: Let me stand here till thou remember it. *(He grins.)*

Juliet: (Laughing in return) I shall forget, to have thee still stand there, remembering how I love thy company.

Romeo: And I'll still stay, to have thee still forget, forgetting any other home but this!

Juliet: (Looking away to the east.) Tis almost morning ....*(She wants to keep Romeo like a pet bird on a string.)* I would have thee gone...and yet no further than a wanton's bird, who lets it hop a little from her hand, like a poor prisoner in his twisted gyves, and with a silk thread plucks it back again, so loving-jealous of his liberty.

Romeo: (Yearning) I would I were thy bird!

Juliet: Sweet, so would I. Yet I should kill thee with much cherishing. *(She blows him a last kiss.)* Good night, good night! Parting is such sweet sorrow that I shall say, "Good night," till it be morrow. *(And very slowly she backs away into the dark.)*

Romeo: Sleep dwell upon thine eyes, peace in thy breast. Would I were sleep and peace, so sweet to rest! *(The enchantment of the nighttime lingers, but a lark's sunrise song recalls him to himself. He is in enemy territory; he must leave unseen. As he starts to climb the Capulet wall, a thought strikes him. He will visit his counselor-priest to seek his aid.)* Hence will I to my ghostly father's cell, his help to crave and my dear hap to tell. *(He climbs over the orchard wall to go to the monastery.)*

Scene 3

(As the early dawn lights the monastery, kindly old Friar Lawrence bustles about his cell room, preparing to gather plants and flowers from the graveyard and fields beyond. On a table are flasks and tubes to distill herbal medicines. Taking up his basket, he speaks to himself.)

Friar: The gray-eyed morn smiles on the frowning night, checkering the eastern clouds with streaks of light. *(He pats his willow-basket.)* Now, ere the sun advance his burning eye, the day to cheer and night's dank dew to dry, I must up-fill this osier-cage of ours with baleful weeds and precious-juiced flowers.

(Looking on the graveyard, he reflects, as Romeo did, on the mixed character of the world.) The earth that's nature's mother is her tomb. What is

her burying grave, that is her womb. And from her womb...children of diverse kind, we, sucking on her natural bosom, find. Many for many virtues excellent, none but for some, and yet...all different!

(Each plant he sees has some hidden good in it, yet often it is mixed with evil when used wrongly.) O, mickle is the powerful grace that lies in plants, herbs, stones, and their true qualities. For naught so vile that on the earth doth live, but to the earth some special good doth give. Nor aught so good but, strained from that fair use, revolts from true birth, stumbling on abuse. Virtue itself turns vice, being misapplied. And vice sometime's by action dignified.

(Romeo enters to hear the Friar's last words about a flower which is both drug and poison, as man's inner nature also is.) Within the infant rind of this small flower, poison hath residence and medicine power. For this, being smelt, with that part cheers each part. Being tasted, slays all senses with the heart. Two such opposing kings encamp them still, in man as well as herbs — grace and rude will. And where the worser is predominant, full soon the canker death eats up that plant!

Romeo: (Smiling with affection) Good morrow, Father.

Friar: (Startled, he gives an automatic blessing in greeting.) Benedicite! What early tongue so sweet saluteth me? *(He looks at Romeo with fond disapproval for being up so early.)* Young son, it

argues a distempered head so soon to bid good-morrow to thy bed. Or, if not so, then here I hit it right...our Romeo hath not been in bed tonight!

Romeo: *(With a happy sigh.)* That last is true. The sweeter rest was mine!

Friar: *(Shocked)* God pardon sin! Wast thou with Rosaline?

Romeo: *(Laughing, for he has forgotten her already.)* With Rosaline, my ghostly father? No! I have forgot that name and that name's woe.

Friar: *(Smiling)* That's my good son! But where hast thou been then?

Romeo: I'll tell thee ere thou ask it me again. *(Poetically and mysteriously referring to love and Cupid's arrows.)* I have been feasting with mine enemy, where, on a sudden, one hath wounded me that's by me wounded.

Friar: *(Wanting everyday speech)* Be plain, good son, and homely in thy drift!

Romeo: Then...plainly know my heart's dear love is set on the fair daughter of rich Capulet! *(The Friar sits on a bench in astonishment, and Romeo sits beside him to explain how Juliet's heart and his are joined, so the Friar must join them in marriage.)* As mine on hers, so hers is set on mine. And all combined, save what thou must combine by holy marriage. When and where and how we met, we wooed, and made exchange of vow, I'll tell thee as we pass. But this I pray...that thou consent to marry us today!

Friar: (Not believing that Romeo's tears over Rosaline have dried so soon.) Holy Saint Francis! What a change is here! Is Rosaline, that thou didst love so dear, so soon forsaken? Jesu Maria! *(He traces the tear-trails down Romeo's blushing cheeks.)* Lo, here upon thy cheek the stain doth sit of an old tear that is not washed off yet.

Romeo: (A little sulky and defensive.) Thou chidest me oft for loving Rosaline.

Friar: (Reminding Romeo of the difference between puppy love and real love.) For doting, not for loving, pupil mine.

Romeo: And badest me bury love.

Friar: Not in a grave to lay one in, another out to have. *(He chuckles, nevertheless.)* But come, young waverer, come go with me. In one respect, I'll thy assistant be... *(Hopefully he thinks the marriage may end the feud.)*...for this alliance may so happy prove, to turn your households' rancor to pure love.

Romeo: (Jumping up) O, let us hence! I stand on sudden haste!

Friar: Wisely and slow. They stumble that run fast! *(As Romeo tugs at his arm eagerly, the gentle old friar goes to make arrangements at the church, quite forgetting his earlier wise words about good things becoming evil when applied wrong. And he is too unworldly to tell Romeo to ask for the help of the Prince, who would undoubtedly approve the wedding as a gesture of peace.)*

Scene 4

(In the plaza, now the sun is up, Benvolio and Mercutio meet to talk over the last night's adventures. They look about for Romeo, who usually joins them.)

Mercutio: Why, where the devil should this Romeo be? Came he not home tonight?

Benvolio: Not to his father's. I spoke with his man.

Mercutio: (Thinking Romeo is still love-sick over the white-skinned, dark-eyed Rosaline.) Why, that same pale hard-hearted wench, that Rosaline, torments him so, that he will sure run mad.

Benvolio: (Worried) Tybalt, the kinsman to old Capulet, hath sent a letter to his father's house.

Mercutio: (Smelling a duel between Tybalt and Romeo.) A challenge, on my life!

Benvolio: Romeo will answer it.

Mercutio: Alas, poor Romeo, he is already dead — stabbed with a white wench's black eye, shot through the ear with a love song. Is he the man to encounter Tybalt?

Benvolio: Why, what is Tybalt? *(He meows scornfully, as cats in medieval fables are named Tybalt- or Tabby-cats.)*

Mercutio: More than Prince of Cats, I can tell you. *(He rises, imitating Tybalt's sleek dancing manner of swordplay.)* O, he's the courageous captain of complements! He fights as you sing pricksong — keeps time, distance and proportion. *(He counts,*

*as if to formal music and then lunges with his
sword.)* One...two...and the third in your bosom!
The very butcher of a silk button! *(He flicks a
button off Benvolio's jacket.)* A duelist, a duelist!
*(He illustrates various fashionable and fancy new
sword attacks.)* Ah, the immortal "passado"! The
"punto reverso"! The "hay"! *(He stamps his foot
as he lunges.)*

Benvolio: The **what**?

*Mercutio: (Walking about in a precise, cat-like fash-
ion.)* The pox of such antic, lisping, affecting
fantasticoes! *(Suddenly he imitates an old, old
man.)* Why, is not this a lamentable thing, grand-
sire, that we should be thus afflicted with these
strange flies, these fashion-mongers, these
"pardona-mi's"! Oh! *(His silly antics stop as he
sees Romeo coming, full of smiles after completing
his wedding arrangements. His friends, though,
think he has spent the night with Rosaline.)*

Benvolio: Here comes Romeo! Here comes Romeo!

Mercutio: Without his roe, like a dried herring! *(He
pretends to be shocked.)* O flesh, flesh, how art
thou fishified! *(He gives Romeo an exaggerated
French greeting to match Romeo's French-style
breeches.)* Signior Romeo, bon jour! There's a
French salutation to your French slop. You gave
us the counterfeit fairly last night.

Romeo: Good morrow to you both. What counterfeit
did I give you?

Mercutio: The slip, sir, the slip.

Romeo: Pardon, good Mercutio. My business was great, and in such a case as mine, a man may strain courtesy.

Mercutio: (Snatching a flower growing by the fountain.) Nay, I am the very pink of courtesy.

Romeo: Pink for flower.

Mercutio: Right! *(He makes an elaborate bow.)*

Romeo: (Taking aim and kicking Mercutio in the rear as he bends.) Why, then is my pump well-flowered!

Mercutio: (Kicking in return as he rattles out wordplay to claim his joking is unique.) Well-said! Follow me this jest now, till thou hast worn out thy pump — that when the single sole of it is worn, the jest may remain, after the wearing, solely singular.

Romeo: (Joking back) O single-soled jest, solely singular for the singleness!

Mercutio: (Pretending to be overcome) Come between us, good Benvolio! My wits faint! *(He collapses on Romeo's shoulder, and they wrestle about in fun.)*

Romeo: (Getting Mercutio in a stranglehold.) Switch and spurs! Switch and spurs, or I'll cry a match!

Mercutio: I will bite thee by the ear!

Romeo: Nay, bite not!

Mercutio: (Breaking up the scuffle, he shouts in joy that Romeo is himself again.) Why, is not this better now than groaning for love? Now art thou sociable. Now art thou Romeo! *(In high spirits, he*

starts to chase Romeo, who accidentally collides with the Nurse. She has entered, followed by stupid Peter.)

Benvolio: Stop there, stop there!

Romeo: Here's goodly gear! *(He distangles himself from the Nurse's billowing veil.)*

Mercutio: A sail, a sail! *(He circles the Nurse, snatching at her veil.)*

Benvolio: (Snatching at Peter's long blouse.) Two, two! A shirt and a smock!

Nurse: (Horrified at their familiarities.) Peter!

Peter: Anon.

Nurse: My fan, Peter. *(Peter gives her the fan, which she uses to cover her face as if she is a beauty pursued by men.)*

Mercutio: (Cat-calling) Good Peter, to hide her face. For her fan's the fairer face!

Nurse: (With attempted dignity) God ye good morrow, gentlemen.

Mercutio: (Saying "good evening" in return.) God ye good-den, fair gentlewoman.

Nurse: (Looking up at the sun to see if it is afternoon yet.) Is it good-den?

Mercutio: Tis no less, I tell ye. For the bawdy hand of the dial is now...upon the prick of noon! *(And he pinches her round bottom as she looks upward.)*

Nurse: (Shocked) Out upon you! What a man are you!

Romeo: (Explaining Mercutio will ruin himself yet.) One, gentlewoman, that God hath made for himself to mar.

Nurse: (With a toothless smile of approval at Romeo.) By my troth, it is well-said, "For himself to mar," quoth he. *(Curbing her anger at Mercutio, she curtsies to the three young men.)* Gentlemen, can any of you tell me where I may find the young Romeo?

Romeo: (Teasing her a little) I can tell you, but young Romeo will be older when you have found him than he was when you sought him. *(At her puzzled look, he introduces himself.)* I am the youngest of that name.

Nurse: (Giving him a nod of approval, as she inspects his handsome appearance.) You say well. If you be he, sir, I desire some confidence with you! *(She takes his arm to lead him away for a private talk, but the others pretend she is a madam from a brothel.)*

Benvolio: She will endite him to some supper!

Mercutio: (With mock horror) A bawd, a bawd, a bawd! So, **ho!** *(He walks about, singing a naughty old song about a gray (hoar) rabbit (hare). The Nurse is furious at the insult.)*

> An old hare hoar
>   And an old hare hoar,
> Is very good meat in Lent.
>   But a hare that is hoar
> Is too much for a score
>   When it hoars ere it be spent!

(To his friend, casually) Romeo, will you come to
your father's? We'll to dinner thither.

Romeo: (Furiously motioning them to leave.) I will
follow you.

*Mercutio: (With a bow to the Nurse, who is red with
rage at his insulting jokes.)* Farewell, ancient
lady. Farewell....*(He kisses his hand to her and
goes off singing, "Lady, lady, lady...." He and
Benvolio disappear into the Montague house,
while the Nurse puffs in anger, and Romeo tries to
soothe her, realizing she is Juliet's messenger.)*

Nurse: (To the vanishing Mercutio) Marry, farewell!
(To Romeo) I pray you, sir, what saucy merchant
was this?

Romeo: A gentleman, Nurse, that loves to hear himself talk, and will speak more in a minute than he
will stand to in a month.

Nurse: And he speak anything against me, I'll take
him down! *(She shakes her fist at the departed
Mercutio.)* And if I cannot, I'll find those that
shall. Scurvy knave! I am none of his flirt-gills! *(To
Peter, in a rage at him too.)* And **thou** must stand
by, too, and suffer every knave to use me at his
pleasure!

Peter: (In his own defense) I saw no man use you at
his pleasure. If I had, my weapon should quickly
have been out, I warrant you. I dare draw as soon
as another man...*(Hesitating, out of cowardice)*
...if I see occasion in a good quarrel and the law on
my side.

Nurse: (Still panting with anger) Now, afore God, I am so vexed that every part about me quivers. Scurvy knave! *(To Romeo, who waits politely.)* Pray you, sir, a word. And as I told you, my young lady bid me inquire you out. *(Romeo sits beside her on a bench, eager to get news of Juliet, but the Nurse first makes sure his intentions are honest.)* What she bid me say, I will keep to myself...but first let me tell ye, if ye should lead her into a "fool's paradise," as they say, it were a very gross kind of behavior, as they say. For the gentlewoman is young. And therefore, if you should "deal double" with her, truly it were an ill thing to be offered to any gentlewoman.

Romeo: (Swearing his good intentions) Nurse, commend me to thy lady and mistress. I protest unto thee....

Nurse: (Interrupting) Good heart, and in faith I will tell her as much. *(Throwing up her hands with glee.)* Lord, Lord, she will be a joyful woman!

Romeo: (His speech still incomplete) What wilt thou tell her, Nurse? Thou dost not mark me.

Nurse: I will tell her, sir, that you do protest...which, as I take it, is a gentlemanlike offer!

Romeo: (Smiling as he outlines the marriage plan, if Juliet can come to the Friar's cell for confession.) Bid her devise some means to come to shrift this afternoon. And there she shall, at Friar Lawrence' cell, be shrived and married. *(He gives the Nurse a piece of gold.)* Here is for thy pains.

Nurse: (Refusing weakly) No, truly, sir. Not a penny!

Romeo: Go to! I say you shall. *(He forces the money into her hand, and she quickly tucks it down the front of her smock.)*

Nurse: This afternoon, sir? Well, she shall be there. *(She rises.)*

Romeo: And stay, good Nurse. *(Making arrangements for a rope-ladder.)* Behind the abbey wall, within this hour, my man shall be with thee and bring thee cords made like a tackled stair. *(The Nurse nods.)* Farewell. Be trusty…*(He pats his money-pouch.)*…and I'll quit thy pains. *(She curtsies with joy at his generosity.)* Farewell. Commend me to thy mistress!

Nurse: Now God in Heaven bless thee! *(She stops on her way out, worried.)* Hark you, sir.

Romeo: What sayst thou, my dear Nurse?

Nurse: (Fearing his servant will tell on them.) Is your man secret? Did you never hear say, "Two may keep counsel, putting one away?"

Romeo: I warrant thee, my man's as true as steel.

Nurse: Well, sir, my mistress is the sweetest lady… O there is a nobleman in town, one Paris…but she, good soul, had as lief see a toad, a very toad as see him! *(She laughs, enjoying her gossip, but Romeo wants to speed her back to Juliet.)*

Romeo: Commend me to thy lady.

Nurse: Ay, a thousand times. *(Romeo almost pushes her towards the Capulet house, but the Nurse calls to her servant.)* Peter!

Peter: Anon. *(He stands at attention, waiting.)*

Nurse: (Motioning for him to go ahead, she starts to stroll about the town like a great lady.) Peter, take my fan and go before!

Scene 5

(In the orchard where Romeo stood beneath her balcony, Juliet waits impatiently for the Nurse to return with news of the wedding arrangements made by Romeo. She bites her lip with worry.)

Juliet: The clock struck nine when I did send the Nurse. In half an hour she promised to return... Perchance she cannot meet him!...That's not so. O, she is lame! *(Wishing that Love's messengers were thought-waves, faster than sunlight.)* Love's heralds should be thoughts, which ten times faster glide than the sun's beams, driving back shadows over louring hills. *(She looks up at the noonday sun.)* Now is the sun upon the highmost hill of this day's journey, and from nine till twelve is three long hours. Yet she is not come! *(Thinking if the Nurse were young, she would bounce back and forth between lovers like a ball.)* Had she affections and warm youthful blood, she would be as swift in motion as a ball. My words would bandy

her to my sweet love, and his to me. But old folks,
many feign as they were dead — unwieldy, slow,
heavy and pale as lead.

*(The Nurse and Peter enter, tired, as if they have
traveled many miles.)* O God, she comes! O honey
Nurse, what news? Hast thou met with him? Send
thy man away!

Nurse: Peter, stay at the gate. *(Peter leaves, and the
Nurse sits on a garden bench wearily with a long
face, teasing Juliet.)*

Juliet: Now, good sweet Nurse...O Lord, why lookest
thou sad? Though news be sad, yet tell them
merrily. If good, thou shamest the music of sweet
news by playing it to me with so sour a face.

Nurse: (Pretending total exhaustion) I am aweary...
give me leave awhile. Fie, how my bones ache!
What a jaunt have I had!

Juliet: I would thou hadst my bones, and I thy news!
(Kneeling and pleading) Nay, come, I pray thee,
speak. Good, good Nurse, speak!

*Nurse: (In a cross voice, though she enjoys keeping
Juliet in suspense.)* Jesu, what haste! Can you not
stay awhile? Do you not see that I am out of
breath?

Juliet: (Desperate) How art thou out of breath, when
thou hast breath to say to me that thou art out of
breath? Is thy news good or bad? Answer to that.
Let me be satisfied...is it good or bad?

Nurse: (Instead of answering, she makes comments on Romeo, especially his good looks.) Well, you have made a simple choice. You know not how to choose a man. Romeo? No, not he. Though his face be better than any man's, yet his leg excels all men's. And for a hand and a foot and a body — though they be not to be talked on! — yet they are past compare. He is not the flower of courtesy, but, I'll warrant him, as gentle as a lamb. Go thy ways, wench! Serve God. *(She sniffs the air.)* What, have you dined at home?

Juliet: No, no. But all this did I know before. What says he of our marriage? What of that?

Nurse: (With a loud shriek) Lord, how my head aches! What a head have I! It beats as it would fall in twenty pieces. *(Juliet jumps up and starts rubbing the Nurse's head, whereupon the old woman wails again.)* My back!...*(Juliet rubs her backbone.)* ...on t'other side...*(Juliet rubs it on the other side.)*...ah, my back, my back! Beshrew your heart for sending me about, to catch my death with jaunting up and down!

Juliet: (Almost in tears from frustration.) In faith, I am sorry that thou art not well. Sweet, sweet, sweet Nurse, tell me...What says my love?

Nurse: (Kindly) Your love says, like an honest gentle-man, and a courteous, and a kind, and a hand-some, and, I warrant, a virtuous...*(She looks about)*...Where is your mother?

Juliet: Where is my mother? *(She motions inside the house, growing almost angry.)* Why, she is within. Where should she be? How oddly thou repliest: "Your love says, like an honest gentleman, 'Where is your mother?'"

Nurse: (Pretending to be angry too.) O God's Lady dear! Are you so hot? Marry, come up, I trow! Is this the poultice for my aching bones? Henceforward do your messages yourself!

Juliet: Here's such a coil! *(Completely defeated, she takes the Nurse's hand gently.)* Come, what says Romeo?

Nurse: Have you got leave to go to shrift today? *(Her old eyes twinkle at the surprise Juliet will find at confession in the old Friar's cell.)*

Juliet: I have.

Nurse: (With a broad grin) Then hie you hence to Friar Lawrence' cell. There stays a husband to make you a wife! *(Juliet, overcome with blushes of joy, hugs the Nurse.)* Now comes the wanton blood up in your cheeks! They'll be in scarlet straight at any news. Hie you to church!

(Juliet rises while the Nurse explains the arrangement for the wedding night.) I must another way, to fetch a ladder, by the which your love must climb a "bird's nest" soon when it is dark. *(With a quick pat, the Nurse hurries the blushing girl away.)* Go! I'll to dinner. Hie you to the cell!

Juliet: (Running joyfully into the house to get her scarf.) Hie to high fortune! Honest Nurse, farewell.

(The Nurse chuckles with happiness, too busy thinking of the wedding to realize the problems the lovers face or to suggest they ask the Prince's aid.)

Scene 6

(In Friar Lawrence's cell, he and Romeo wait for Juliet. In Romeo's hand is a wreath of flowers for his bride. The Friar prays that God approve the marriage and that the future will be happy.)

Friar: So smile the Heavens upon this holy act, that after-hours with sorrow chide us not!

Romeo: Amen, amen! *(All he wants is to be married, and then even death will not matter.)* Do thou but close our hands with holy words. Then love-devouring Death do what he dare. It is enough I may but call her mine!

Friar: (Trying to quiet Romeo's enthusiasm.) These violent delights have violent ends. Therefore, love moderately! Long love doth so. *(Juliet enters with a rush into Romeo's welcoming arms.)* Here comes the lady.

Juliet: (Remembering her manners somewhat tardily, she curtsies to the Friar as she blushes.) Good even to my ghostly confessor.

Friar: Romeo shall thank thee, daughter, for us both.

Friar: You shall not stay alone till Holy
Church incorporate two in one!

Romeo: (*About to kiss her*) Ah, Juliet....(*But the old Friar raises his hand and motions them towards the church door.*)

Friar: Come, come with me, and we will make short work. For, by your leaves, you shall not stay alone till Holy Church incorporate two in one.

    (*Juliet puts the wreath of flowers on her head. And hand-in-hand she and Romeo enter the church door.*)

ACT III

Scene 1

(In the early afternoon of the same day, the heat of mid-July beats down on the plaza. Mercutio, Benvolio and their servants lounge about, feeling lazy and irritable, still suffering the effects of the Capulet's party the night before. Benvolio senses trouble in the air.)

Benvolio: I pray thee, good Mercutio, let's retire. The day is hot, the Capulets abroad, and, if we meet, we shall not escape a brawl, for now, these hot days, is the mad blood stirring. *(He makes a movement towards the Montague house, but Mercutio refuses to budge, accusing calm Benvolio of being quick-tempered.)*

Mercutio: Come, come, thou art as hot a Jack in thy mood as any in Italy. Why, thou wilt quarrel with a man that hath a hair more or a hair less in his beard than thou hast. Thou wilt quarrel with a man for cracking nuts, having no other reason but because thou hast hazel eyes. Thy head is as full of quarrels as an egg is full of meat. Thou hast quarreled with a man for coughing in the street, because he hath wakened thy dog that hath lain asleep in the sun. And yet thou wilt tutor me from quarreling! *(As he laughs, Tybalt and other Capulets enter, anxious for revenge on Romeo for coming to their feast.)*

Benvolio: By my head, here comes the Capulets.

Mercutio: By my heel, I care not.

Tybalt: (To an attendant) Follow me close, for I will speak to them. *(He makes a bow to Benvolio and Mercutio.)* Gentlemen, a word with one of you. *(Benvolio, the peace-maker, bows back. Mercutio, however, smiles a slow, teasing smile.)*

Mercutio: And but one word with one of us? Couple it with something…Make it a word and a blow!

Tybalt: You shall find me apt enough to that, sir, and you will give me occasion.

Mercutio: (Needling him) Could you not **take** some occasion without giving?

Tybalt: (Trying to control his temper, he states his main subject.) Mercutio, thou consortest with Romeo….

Mercutio: (Purposely misunderstanding, he makes puns with "consort," and "concert.") Consort? What, dost thou make us minstrels? And thou make minstrels of us, look to hear nothing but discords. *(He waves his sword like a violin bow.)* Here's my fiddlestick! Here's that shall make you dance. *(A snort of contempt)* Zounds…"consort"!

Benvolio: (To avoid trouble, he suggests they move.) We talk here in the public haunt of men. Either withdraw unto some private place, or else depart. Here all eyes gaze on us.

Mercutio: (Lazily waving his sword at Tybalt.) Men's eyes were made to look, and let them gaze. I will not budge for no man's pleasure, I.

(Into the plaza comes Romeo, carrying a flower from Juliet's wedding wreath, a smiling married man. Tybalt sees him and purrs like a tiger.)

Tybalt: (To Mercutio) Well, peace be with you, sir. Here comes my man. *(Stepping in front of Romeo, who grins at him now they are cousins by marriage, Tybalt flings an insult.)* Romeo, the love I bear thee can afford no better term than this: thou art a villain!

Romeo: (Instead of drawing his sword, he answers mildly.) Tybalt, the reason that I have to love thee doth much excuse the appertaining rage to such a greeting. Villain am I none. Therefore, farewell. I see thou knowest me not. *(He gently tries to go past the angry Capulet.)*

Tybalt: Boy, this shall not excuse the injuries that thou hast done me. *(Romeo walks on.)* Therefore, turn and draw.

Romeo: (Peaceably) I do protest I never injured thee, but love thee better than thou canst devise, till thou shalt know the reason of my love. And so, good Capulet, which name I tender as dearly as mine own, be satisfied. *(He bows, leaving Tybalt speechless and Mercutio in a rage that he seems so cowardly.)*

Mercutio: O calm, dishonorable, vile submission! *(Crying out a fencing term to Tybalt, he springs to*

attack him for Romeo's sake.) "Alla stocatta" carries it away! Tybalt, you rat-catcher, will you walk? *(He brings his rapier up.)*

Tybalt: *(Hesitating, as his quarrel is with Montagues, not with kinsmen of the Prince like Mercutio.)* What wouldst thou have with me?

Mercutio: Good King of Cats, nothing but one of your nine lives! Will you pluck your sword out? Make haste!

Tybalt: I am for you! *(With a hiss, his sword is out, ready.)*

Romeo: *(In distress)* Gentle Mercutio, put thy rapier up!

Mercutio: Come, sir, your "passado"! *(He and Tybalt fight, Mercutio with energy and flair, and Tybalt with mathematical excellence.)*

Romeo: Draw, Benvolio! Beat down their weapons. Gentlemen, for shame! *(Desperately he tries to stop the duel.)* Tybalt, Mercutio...the Prince expressly hath forbid this bandying in Verona streets. Hold, Tybalt! *(He tries to keep Mercutio back.)* Good Mercutio!

(Mercutio is hampered by Romeo's arm, and Tybalt takes advantage of their struggle. His blade glides into Mercutio's chest and out in an instant. He backs away and Mercutio sinks to the ground, his face amazed. Then, realizing what he has done, Tybalt runs off. Slowly Mercutio puts his hand to his side, where the blood is welling through.)

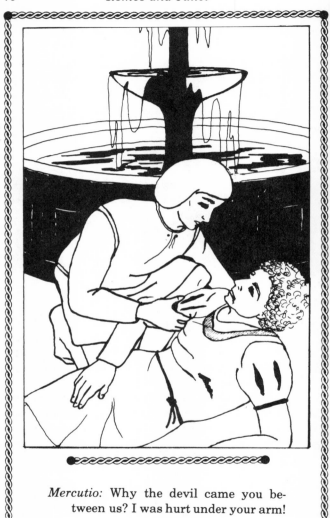

Mercutio: Why the devil came you between us? I was hurt under your arm!

Mercutio: I am hurt. A plague on both your houses! *(Bloody foam comes from his lips, and he wipes it off and looks at it.)* I am sped. *(Looking about for Tybalt.)* Is he gone and hath nothing? *(He lies back on the fountain steps, where he jokingly had "played dead" before. Benvolio runs to help him.)*

Benvolio: What, art thou hurt?

Mercutio: Ay, ay, a scratch, a scratch. *(He winces at the pain.)* Marry, tis enough. Where is my page? *(His Page comes forward.)* Go, villain, fetch a surgeon. *(The Page runs off. Romeo stands in a daze, not realizing fully what has happened.)*

Romeo: Courage, man! The hurt cannot be much.

Mercutio: (Knowing he has a death-wound.) No, tis not so deep as a well, nor so wide as a church door, but tis enough. Twill serve. *(With a last joke, he grins comically as death creeps through him.)* Ask for me tomorrow, and you shall find me a "grave" man. I am peppered, I warrant, for this world. *(In a fury to Romeo, who kneels beside him.)* A plague on both your houses! *(Cursing Tybalt)* Zounds, a dog, a rat, a mouse, a cat... to scratch a man to death. A braggart, a rogue, a villain, that fights by the book of arithmetic! *(To Romeo, with desperate affection.)* Why the devil came you between us? I was hurt under your arm!

Romeo: (Overwhelmed with guilt) I thought all for the best.

Mercutio: Help me into some house, Benvolio, or I shall faint. *(To all the Montagues and Capulets he*

shouts last bitter words.) A plague on both your houses! They have made worms' meat of me. *(He puts his hand to his side in agony.)* I have it, and soundly too. Your houses!

(As Benvolio helps him into the Montague house, Romeo looks after his jolly young friend whose death he has caused. He speaks to himself in despair.)

Romeo: This gentleman, the Prince's near ally, my very friend, hath got this mortal hurt in my behalf...my reputation stained with Tybalt's slander...Tybalt, that an hour hath been my kinsman...*(He picks up Juliet's wedding flower, which has fallen to the ground in a pool of blood.)* O sweet Juliet, thy beauty hath made me effeminate!

Benvolio: *(Returning in tears)* O Romeo, Romeo! Brave Mercutio's dead! *(They stare at each other, not wanting to believe it is so. At this moment Tybalt returns, his sword still drawn, a frown still on his dark face.)* Here comes the furious Tybalt back again!

Romeo: *(Roused from grief into rage.)* Alive in triumph, and Mercutio slain? *(Dropping the flower, he draws his sword and brandishes it in the air as he shouts out a challenge.)* Now, Tybalt, take the "villain" back again that late thou gavest me! *(He gestures towards Heaven, where his merry friend has gone.)* For Mercutio's soul is but a little way above our heads. Either thou or I — or both — must go with him!

Tybalt: (Coldly furious) Thou, wretched boy, shalt with him hence!

Romeo: This shall determine that. *(He lunges at Tybalt, and they fight fiercely. Tybalt's elegant precision is no match for Romeo's rage. Up and down the plaza they fence, sparks flying from the steel. Bystanders run off, shouting for the city guards. At last, with a fierce lunge that beats down Tybalt's guard, Romeo runs him through the heart. Panting, he crouches over Tybalt's corpse.)*

Benvolio: (In alarm) Romeo, away, be gone! The citizens are up, and Tybalt slain! *(Romeo rises but does not move away.)* Stand not amazed. *(He tries to shake Romeo out of his stupor.)* The Prince will doom thee death if thou art taken. Hence, be gone, away!

Romeo: (Putting his hands over his face in misery at his bad luck.) O, I am Fortune's fool!

Benvolio: Why dost thou stay? *(Romeo stumbles off just before the Citizens and Officers enter.)*

1 Officer: (To Benvolio) Which way ran he that killed Mercutio? Tybalt, that murderer, which way ran he?

Benvolio: (Pointing) There lies that Tybalt.

1 Officer: (Stupidly arresting the corpse) Up, sir, go with me. I charge thee in the Prince's name, obey!

(Summoned by the watchmen, the Prince enters with Old Montague, Old Capulet, their wives and a crowd. The Prince calls out in great anger.)

Prince: Where are the vile beginners of this fray?

Benvolio: O noble Prince,...*(Pointing to Tybalt)*...
there lies the man, slain by young Romeo, that
slew thy kinsman, brave Mercutio.

*Lady Capulet: (Kneeling in grief over Tybalt's hand-
some corpse.)* Tybalt, my cousin! O my brother's
child! O Prince! O Husband! O, the blood is spilt of
my dear kinsman! *(In a fury of revenge.)* Prince, as
thou art true, for blood of ours, shed blood of
Montague! *(She throws herself on the corpse.)* O
cousin, cousin!

Prince: Benvolio, who began this bloody fray?

Benvolio: Tybalt, here slain, whom Romeo's hand did
slay. Romeo, that spoke him fair, bid him bethink
how nice the quarrel was, and urged withal your
high displeasure. All this — uttered with gentle
breath, calm look, knees humbly bowed — could
not take truce with Tybalt, deaf to peace, but that
he tilts with piercing steel at bold Mercutio's
breast — who, all as hot, turns deadly point to
point. Romeo...he cries aloud, "Hold, friends!
Friends, part!" underneath whose arm an envious
thrust from Tybalt hit the life of stout Mercutio,
and then Tybalt fled. But by and by comes back to
Romeo, and to it they go like lightning. For, ere I
could draw to part them, was stout Tybalt slain.
And, as he fell, did Romeo turn and fly. This is the
truth, or let Benvolio die.

Lady Capulet: (Shaking her fist at Benvolio.) He is a
kinsman to the Montague. Affection makes him
false...he speaks not true. Some twenty of them

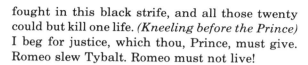

fought in this black strife, and all those twenty could but kill one life. *(Kneeling before the Prince)* I beg for justice, which thou, Prince, must give. Romeo slew Tybalt. Romeo must not live!

Prince: Romeo slew him. He slew Mercutio. Who now the price of his dear blood doth owe?

Montague: Not Romeo, Prince. He was Mercutio's friend. His fault concludes but what the law should end, the life of Tybalt.

Prince: (Giving judgment on Romeo) And for that offence, immediately we do exile him hence. *(Lady Montague cries out at the sentence of banishment, but the Prince holds up his hand for silence.)* I will be deaf to pleading and excuses, nor tears nor prayers. Therefore use none. Let Romeo hence in haste, else, when he's found, that hour is his last. *(To the guards)* Bear hence this body and attend our will. *(To the Montagues)* Mercy but murders, pardoning those that kill!

(Sadly the crowd disperses, and with these deaths, unknown to all, Romeo and Juliet's only connection with the Prince — his kinsman, Mercutio — is broken. But even if the Prince knew of the marriage now, he could not approve it. Tybalt's death and Romeo's banishment set the seal of doom upon the lovers.)

Scene 2

(In the orchard, Juliet waits for her wedding night, ignorant of the fatal street brawl. Excited and happy,

*she urges the sun to hasten across the sky and bring
her wedding night with Romeo.)*

Juliet: Gallop apace, you fiery-footed steeds, towards
   Phoebus' lodging! Spread thy close curtain, love-
   performing night, that Romeo leap to these arms,
   untalked of and unseen. Come, gentle night.
   Come, loving, black-browed night. Give me my
   Romeo! *(She smiles, playing with fantasies of the
   future.)* And when he shall die, take him and cut
   him out in little stars, and he will make the face of
   heaven so fine that all the world will be in love
   with night and pay no worship to the garish sun.

   (She sighs, yearning for married love.) O, I have
   bought the mansion of a love, but not possessed it.
   And though I am sold, not yet enjoyed. So tedious
   is this day as is the night before some festival to an
   impatient child that hath new robes and may not
   wear them.

   (A sound makes her turn.) O, here comes my
   Nurse. *(The Nurse enters, wringing her hands,
   with the rope ladder wrapped in her apron.)* And
   she brings news. Now, Nurse, what news? What
   hast thou there? The cords that Romeo bid thee
   fetch?

Nurse: Ay, ay, the cords. *(She throws them down.)*

Juliet: Ay me! What news? Why dost thou wring thy
   hands?

Nurse: (Sitting and rocking back and forth with grief.)
   Ah, well-a-day! He's dead, he's dead, he's dead! We

are undone, lady, we are undone! Alack the day!
He's gone, he's killed, he's dead!

*Juliet: (With the thought that Romeo is dead because
Fate is jealous of their happiness.)* Can Heaven be
so envious?

Nurse: O Romeo, Romeo! Who ever would have
thought it? Romeo!

*Juliet: (Trying to shake the news from her, half in
anger.)* What devil art thou that dost torment me
thus? This torture should be roared in dismal Hell.
Hath Romeo slain himself?

Nurse: I saw the wound. I saw it with mine eyes — God
save the mark! — here on his manly breast. *(She
touches her heart.)* A piteous corpse, a bloody
piteous corpse! Pale, pale as ashes, all bedaubed in
blood, all in gore-blood.

Juliet: (As she turns away, numb with sorrow.) O
break, my heart!

Nurse: O Tybalt, Tybalt, the best friend I had! O courteous Tybalt! Honest gentleman! That ever I
should live to see thee dead!

Juliet: (Confused) What storm is this that blows so
contrary? Is Romeo slaughtered, and is Tybalt
dead? My dear-loved cousin, and my dearer lord?

Nurse: Tybalt is gone, and Romeo banished. Romeo
that killed him — he is banished!

Juliet: (Starting back with horror) O God! Did Romeo's
hand shed Tybalt's blood?

Nurse: It did, it did! Alas the day, it did!

Juliet: (Lashing out in fury at Romeo, her handsome lover who has proved evil, by killing her favorite cousin.) O serpent heart, hid with a flowering face! Did ever dragon keep so fair a cave? Beautiful tyrant! Fiend angelical! Dove-feathered raven! Wolvish-ravening lamb! O, that deceit should dwell in such a gorgeous palace!

Nurse: There's no trust, no faith, no honesty in men! *(Her old hands tremble, and she calls for brandy.)* Give me some aqua-vitae! These griefs, these woes, these sorrows make me old. *(Shaking her head)* Shame come to Romeo!

Juliet: (Quick in her love's defense.) Blistered be thy tongue for such a wish! He was not born to shame. O, what a beast was I to chide at him!

Nurse: Will you speak well of him that killed your cousin?

Juliet: Shall I speak ill of him that is my husband? *(With shame, as if to Romeo in apology.)* Ah, poor my lord, what tongue shall smooth thy name when I, thy three-hours wife, have mangled it? *(She breaks into weeping.)* But wherefore, villain, didst thou kill my cousin? *(She finds her own answer.)* That villain cousin would have killed my husband. Back, foolish tears! My husband lives, that Tybalt would have slain. And Tybalt's dead, that would have slain my husband. All this is comfort — wherefore weep I then?

(She wipes the tears off with the back of her hand but stops in mid-action.) Some word there was, worser than Tybalt's death, that murdered me. I would forget it...but O, it presses to my memory. "Tybalt is dead, and Romeo...banished." That "banished," that one word "banished" hath slain ten thousand Tybalts. Tybalt's death was woe enough if it had ended there. "Romeo is banished" — to speak that word is father, mother, Tybalt, Romeo, Juliet — all slain, all dead. "Romeo is banished!" *(With a sigh, she looks about, as if to pick up the threads of life again.)* Where is my father and my mother, Nurse?

Nurse: Weeping and wailing over Tybalt's corpse. Will you go to them? I will bring you thither.

Juliet: Wash they his wounds with tears? Mine shall be spent — when theirs are dry — for Romeo's banishment. *(She gives the Nurse the rope-ladder.)* Take up those cords. Poor ropes...he made you for a highway to my bed. But I, a maid, die maiden-widowed. Come, cords. Come, Nurse. *(She starts to leave, sadly, much older already.)* I'll to my "wedding" bed. And Death, not Romeo, take my maidenhead!

Nurse: (Shocked into action by Juliet's despair) Hie to your chamber. I'll find Romeo to comfort you. Hark ye...your Romeo **will** be here at night! I'll to him...he is hid at Lawrence' cell.

Juliet: O, find him! *(Roused from her sorrow, she takes off a great ring and hands it to the Nurse.)* Give this ring to my true knight, and bid him come to take his last farewell. *(With mixed grief and joy, she watches the Nurse bustle off to seek Romeo.)*

Scene 3

(In Friar Lawrence's cell, the old priest hurries in with news from the city. He calls through the doorway of the church to Romeo, who has taken sanctuary there, the one place the Prince's officers cannot arrest him.)

Friar: Romeo, come forth! Come forth, thou fearful man!

Romeo: (Entering from the church, where, shortly before, he and Juliet were married.) Father, what news?

Friar: I bring thee tidings of the Prince's doom.

Romeo: What less than Doomsday is the Prince's doom?

Friar: Not body's death, but body's banishment.

Romeo: (Growing paler) Ha, banishment? Be merciful...say, "Death." Do not say, "Banishment"!

Friar: Hence from Verona art thou banished. *(Romeo sinks weakly on a bench — he has lost his love, his home, his friends, his entire life as he knows it.)* Be patient, for the world is broad and wide.

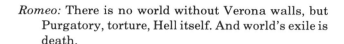

Romeo: There is no world without Verona walls, but Purgatory, torture, Hell itself. And world's exile is death.

Friar: O deadly sin! O rude unthankfulness! Thy fault our law calls death. But the kind Prince, taking thy part, hath rushed aside the law, and turned that black word "death" to "banishment." This is dear mercy, and thou seest it not.

Romeo: Tis torture, and not mercy. *(He looks out toward the city.)* Heaven is here, where Juliet lives. And every cat and dog and little mouse, every unworthy thing, live here in Heaven and may look on her. But Romeo may not. "Banished"? O Friar, the damned use that word in Hell. Howling attends it.

Friar: Thou mad man, hear me a little speak!

Romeo: O, thou wilt speak again of banishment.

Friar: O, then I see that madmen have no ears.

Romeo: Thou canst not speak of that thou dost not feel. *(He tries to explain to the saintly old man.)* Wert thou as young as I, Juliet thy love, an hour but married, Tybalt murdered, doting like me, and like me banished, then mightst thou speak. *(He cries and sinks to the pavement, holding his head as if dying.)* Then mightst thou tear thy hair and fall upon the ground, as I do now, taking the measure of an un-made grave. *(He lies unmoving, as someone knocks at the cell door.)*

Friar: Arise, one knocks. Good Romeo, hide thyself.

Romeo: Not I. *(The knocking continues.)*

Friar: Hark, how they knock! *(Calls)* Who's there? *(To the youth)* Romeo, arise! Thou wilt be taken! *(He tugs at the boy, who remains lying still, as he calls to the visitor.)* Stay awhile! *(To Romeo)* Stand up...run to my study. *(To the person who knocks.)* By and by! *(To Romeo, scolding)* God's will, what simpleness is this? *(To the visitor)* I come, I come! *(More knocking)* Who knocks so hard? Whence come you? What's your will? *(He opens the door a crack to reveal the Nurse.)*

Nurse: Let me come in, and you shall know my errand. I come from Lady Juliet.

Friar: (Standing aside to let her enter.) Welcome then.

Nurse: O holy Friar, O, tell me, holy Friar, where is my lady's lord? Where's Romeo?

Friar: There on the ground, with his own tears made drunk.

Nurse: O, he is even in my mistress' case! Even so lies she, blubbering and weeping, weeping and blubbering. *(She shakes Romeo.)* Stand up, stand up! Stand, and you be a man. For Juliet's sake, for her sake, rise and stand! *(Romeo moans.)* Why should you fall into so deep an "O"?

Romeo: (Rising) Nurse...

Nurse: (Patting him) Ah sir, ah sir!

Romeo: Speakest thou of Juliet? How is it with her? Doth not she think me an old murderer? Where is she? And how doth she?

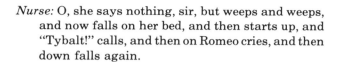

Nurse: O, she says nothing, sir, but weeps and weeps, and now falls on her bed, and then starts up, and "Tybalt!" calls, and then on Romeo cries, and then down falls again.

Romeo: As if that name did murder her... *(He looks at his hand.)*...as that name's cursed hand murdered her kinsman. O, tell me, Friar, tell me in what vile part of this anatomy doth my name lodge? *(He draws his dagger to stab himself to be rid of his name, but the Nurse snatches the weapon from him.)*

Friar: Hold thy desperate hand! Art thou a man? Thy form cries out thou art. Thy tears are womanish! Thy wild acts denote the unreasonable fury of a beast! Thou hast amazed me. By my holy order, I thought thy disposition better tempered. Hast thou slain Tybalt? Wilt thou slay thyself? And slay thy lady that in thy life lives, by doing damned hate upon thyself?

(He puts his arm kindly around the half-crazed youth.) What, rouse thee, man! Thy Juliet is alive. There art thou happy. Tybalt would kill thee, but thou slewest Tybalt. There art thou happy too. The law, that threatened death, becomes thy friend and turns it to exile. There art thou happy. A pack of blessings light upon thy back! Take heed, take heed!

(He pushes Romeo towards the door. Outside, the evening falls.) Go, get thee to thy love, as was decreed. Ascend her chamber, hence, and comfort her. *(Warning him to leave quickly for nearby*

*Mantua, where he is to wait further develop-
ments.)* But look thou stay not till the watch be set,
for then thou canst not pass to Mantua, where
thou shalt live till we can find a time to blaze your
marriage, reconcile your friends, beg pardon of the
Prince, and call thee back with twenty hundred
thousand times more joy than thou wentst forth in
lamentation.
*(Romeo smiles a little and wipes away his tears.
The Friar speaks to the Nurse.)* Go before, Nurse.
Commend me to thy lady, and bid her hasten all
the house to bed. Romeo is coming!

Nurse: (Full of admiration for the wise Friar.) O Lord,
I could have stayed here all the night to hear good
counsel. O, what learning is! *(To Romeo)* My lord,
I'll tell my lady you will come.

Romeo: Do so!

Nurse: Here, sir, a ring she bid me give you, sir. Make
haste, for it grows very late. *(She gives him the
ring and leaves.)*

Romeo: (Putting the ring to his lips.) How well my
comfort is revived by this!

Friar: Go hence, good night! Either be gone before the
watch be set, or by the break of day disguised from
hence. Sojourn in Mantua. *(Planning to use
Romeo's servant as a go-between.)* I'll find out
your man, and he shall signify from time to time
every good hap to you that chances here. Give me
thy hand. Tis late. Farewell! Good night!

Romeo: Farewell! *(With a parting hug, he leaves to
go to Juliet.)*

Scene 4

(In a room in Capulet's house, Old Capulet and his wife talk with County Paris, who has come to offer his sympathy and continue his suit to marry Juliet. Capulet explains he has had no time to talk to Juliet with all of the troubles of the day. It is very late at night.)

Capulet: Things have fallen out, sir, so unluckily that we have had no time to move our daughter. Look you, she loved her kinsman Tybalt dearly, and so did I. *(He sighs philosophically.)* Well, we were born to die. *(In a friendly voice to the young man.)* Tis very late. She'll not come down tonight.

Paris: These times of woe afford no time to woo. *(To Lady Capulet)* Madam, good night. Commend me to your daughter.

Lady Capulet: I will, and know her mind early tomorrow.

Capulet: (Anxious to see Juliet happily married in times when death comes so suddenly, and there is no adult male in the family now other than himself.) Sir Paris, I think she will be ruled in all respects by me. Nay, more...I doubt it not. Wife, go you to her ere you go to bed. Acquaint her here of my son Paris' love and bid her — mark you me? — on Wednesday next...but soft, what day is this?

Paris: Monday, my lord.

Capulet: Monday! Ha, ha! Well, Wednesday is too soon. On Thursday let it be! On Thursday, tell her, she shall be married to this noble earl. *(To Paris)* Will you be ready? Do you like this haste? We'll keep no great ado...a friend or two. For, hark you, Tybalt being slain so late, it may be thought we held him carelessly, being our kinsman. Therefore we'll have some half a dozen friends, and there an end. But what say you to Thursday?

Paris: (Overjoyed) My lord, I would that Thursday were tomorrow!

Capulet: Well, get you gone. On Thursday be it then. *(To his wife)* Go you to Juliet ere you go to bed. Prepare her, wife, against this wedding day. *(To Paris as he leaves.)* Farewell, my lord. *(To a servant)* Light to my chamber, ho! *(The servant takes a torch to lead him through the dark hallways, and Capulet yawns.)* It is so very late that we may call it early by and by. *(To his wife, who stands astonished at the wedding news.)* Good night!

Scene 5

(In the early dawn, about four in the morning, Romeo and Juliet look from her chamber to the balcony overlooking the garden and orchard. A bird sings, and Juliet, desperately trying to keep Romeo for a few more minutes, pretends the bird is a nightingale and not the early-morning lark, which would be a signal that Romeo must leave or die.)

Juliet: Wilt thou be gone? It is not yet near day. It was the nightingale and not the lark that pierced the

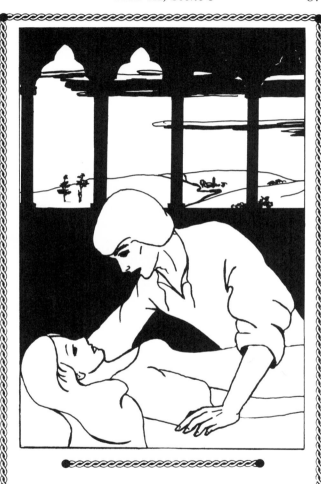

Romeo: I must be gone and live, or stay and die.

fearful hollow of thine ear. Nightly she sings on yon pomegranate tree. Believe me, love, it was the nightingale.

Romeo: It was the lark, the herald of the morn, no nightingale. *(He sadly points to the faint light in the far sky.)* Look, love, what envious streaks do lace the severing clouds in yonder east. *(He watches the stars fade.)* Night's candles are burnt out, and jocund day stands tiptoe on the misty mountaintops. I must be gone and live, or stay and die. *(He kisses her gently.)*

Juliet: *(She turns his face away from the sky.)* Yond light is not daylight...I know it, I. It is some meteor that the sun exhales, to be to thee this night a torchbearer, and light thee on thy way to Mantua. *(She folds him in her arms.)* Therefore stay yet. Thou needst not to be gone.

Romeo: *(Smiling as he buries his face in her hair, pretending to agree.)* Let me be taken. Let me be put to death. I am content, so thou wilt have it so. I'll say yon gray is not the morning's eye. Nor that is not the lark whose notes do beat the vaulty heaven so high above our heads. I have more care to stay than will to go. Come, Death, and welcome! Juliet wills it so. How is it, my soul? *(He embraces her.)* Let's talk. It is not day.

Juliet: *(In agony that he will be arrested.)* It is, it is! Hie hence, be gone, away! It is the lark that sings so out of tune, straining harsh discords and unpleasing sharps. *(She denies the old saying that* the lark joyfully divides the night and morn.) Some say the lark makes sweet division. This doth not so, for she divideth us. O, now be gone! *(She pushes him to the balcony rail.)* More light and light it grows!

Romeo: More light and light...more dark and dark our woes.

Nurse: (Entering hurriedly) Madam!

Juliet: Nurse?

Nurse: Your lady mother is coming to your chamber. The day is broke. Be wary...look about! *(She leaves to forestall Lady Capulet.)*

Juliet: Then, window...let day in, and let life out. *(She goes to his arms for the last time.)*

Romeo: Farewell, farewell! One kiss, and I'll descend. *(They kiss lovingly, desperately. As he climbs down the rope ladder to the ground, Juliet leans over the balcony railing, her hand still reaching toward him.)*

Juliet: Art thou gone so, my lord, my love, my friend? I must hear from thee every day in the hour, for in a minute there are many days.

Romeo: Farewell! I will omit no opportunity that may convey my greetings, love, to thee.

Juliet: O, thinkst thou we shall ever meet again? *(The tears well up in her eyes.)*

Romeo: I doubt it not. *(He smiles to think how they will talk about it in later years.)* And all these woes shall serve for sweet discourses in our time to come.

Juliet: (Starting back in horror as she sees Romeo below in the ghostly light.) O God, I have an ill-divining soul! Methinks I see thee, now thou art below, as one dead in the bottom of a tomb! Either my eyesight fails, or thou lookest pale.

Romeo: And trust me, love, in my eye so do you. Dry sorrow drinks our blood. Adieu, adieu! *(He climbs quickly over the garden wall to flee to Mantua.)*

Juliet: (As she kneels to pray for good luck.) O Fortune, Fortune! All men call thee fickle. **Be** fickle, Fortune, for then I hope thou wilt not keep him long, but send him back....

(Wiping away her tears, she goes to her chamber, where her mother enters. Lady Capulet, tired from having been up all night making funeral arrangements, tends to be a bit short with Juliet's sorrow, apparently for Tybalt's death.)

Lady Capulet: Ho, daughter, are you up?

Juliet: Who is it that calls? *(She wipes her eyes again.)* It is my lady mother. Is she not down so late or up so early?

Lady Capulet: (Looking closely at the girl's tear-stained face.) Why, how now, Juliet?

Juliet: Madam, I am not well.

Lady Capulet: Evermore weeping for your cousin's death? What, wilt thou wash him from his grave with tears? And if thou couldst, thou couldst not make him live. Therefore, have done. *(With a touch of scorn for the stupidity of too much mourning.)* Some grief shows much of love, but much of grief shows still some want of wit.

Juliet: I cannot choose but ever weep the friend.

Lady Capulet: (Briskly) But now I'll tell thee joyful tidings, girl.

Juliet: And joy comes well in such a needy time. What are they, I beseech your ladyship?

Lady Capulet: Well, well, thou hast a careful father, child...one who, to put thee from thy heaviness, hath sorted out a sudden day of joy.

Juliet: (Smiling a little at her father's loving care.) Madam, in happy time! What day is that?

Lady Capulet: (Smiling also) Marry, my child, early next Thursday morn, the gallant, young and noble gentleman, the County Paris, at Saint Peter's Church, shall happily make thee there a joyful bride! *(She clasps her hands with approval, but Juliet whirls away in horror and anger.)*

Juliet: Now, by Saint Peter's Church and Peter too, he shall **not** make me there a joyful bride! *(She searches for reasons to postpone the marriage.)* I wonder at this haste, that I must wed ere he that should be husband comes to woo. I pray you, tell my lord and father, madam, I will not marry yet.

And when I do, I swear it shall be Romeo, whom you know I hate, rather than Paris. These are news indeed! *(She bursts into fresh tears from overstrained nerves.)*

Lady Capulet: (Coldly) Here comes your father. Tell him so yourself, and see how he will take it at your hands.

Capulet: (Entering with the Nurse) How now, girl? What, still in tears? Evermore showering? How now, wife? Have you delivered to her our decree?

Lady Capulet: Ay, sir, but she will none. She gives you thanks. *(With much disgust at her ungrateful daughter.)* I would the fool were married to her grave!

Capulet: (A little slow to comprehend Juliet's refusal of Paris.) Soft! Take me with you, take me with you, wife. How? Will she none? Doth she not give us thanks? Is she not proud? Doth she not count her blest, unworthy as she is, that we have wrought so worthy a gentleman to be her bridegroom?

Juliet: Not proud you have, but thankful that you have. Proud can I never be of what I hate, but thankful even for hate that is meant love.

Capulet: (Beginning to sputter with anger.) How now, how now, chop-logic? What is this? "Proud"... and "I thank you"... and "I thank you not"... and yet "not proud"? Mistress minion you, thank me no thankings, nor proud me no prouds. *(He shakes his fist at her warningly.)* But fettle your fine joints against Thursday next to go with Paris to

Saint Peter's Church, or I will drag thee on a hurdle thither. *(He starts to curse her.)* Out, you green-sickness carrion! Out, you baggage! You tallow-face!

Lady Capulet: (Irritated at her husband's over-reaction.) Fie, fie! What, are you mad?

Juliet: (Kneeling) Good father, I beseech you on my knees, hear me with patience but to speak a word!

Capulet: Hang thee, young baggage! Disobedient wretch! I tell thee what...get thee to church on Thursday or never after look me in the face! Speak not! Reply not! Do not answer me! *(His hands open and shut with rage.)* My fingers itch! *(He shouts at his wife.)* Wife, we scarce thought us blest that God had lent us but this only child. But now I see this one is one too much, and that we have a curse in having her. Out on her, hilding!

Nurse: (Protesting) God in Heaven bless her! You are to blame, my lord, to rate her so!

Capulet: And why, my Lady Wisdom? Hold your tongue, Good Prudence. Go!

Nurse: I speak no treason.

Capulet: (Tearing at his beard) O, **God!**

Nurse: May not one speak?

Capulet: Peace, you mumbling fool!

Lady Capulet: You are too hot!

Capulet: (Furious that he is not appreciated as a good father.) God's bread! It makes me mad. Day, night,

late, early, at home, abroad, alone, in company,
waking or sleeping — still my care hath been to
have her matched! And having now provided a
gentleman of princely parentage, youthful and
nobly trained, stuffed, as they say, with honorable
parts — and then to have a wretched puling fool to
answer,...*(He mimics her.)*..."I'll not wed — I
cannot love — I am too young — I pray you,
pardon me"!

*(He threatens to throw her out of the house if she
refuses.)* But, and you will not wed, you shall not
house with me! Look to it...think on it...Thursday
is near. And you be mine, I'll give you to my friend.
And you be not...hang, beg, starve, die in the
street, for what is mine shall never do thee good!
Trust to it! Bethink you! *(He stamps off, huffing
with rage.)*

Juliet: (A plea to her mother.) O sweet my mother, cast
me not away! Delay this marriage for a month, a
week. Or if you do not, make the bridal bed in that
dim monument where Tybalt lies.

*Lady Capulet: (Speaking coldly as she leaves her dis-
obedient child.)* Talk not to me, for I'll not speak a
word. Do as thou wilt, for I have done with thee.
(With a sniff, she departs.)

Juliet: (Turning to her dearest friend.) O God!...O
Nurse, how shall this be prevented? My husband
is on earth, my faith in Heaven. Comfort me!
Counsel me! What sayst thou? Has thou not a
word of joy? Some comfort, Nurse! *(She creeps into
the Nurse's arms, and the old woman pats her
lovingly as she thinks.)*

Nurse: (With an attempt to make the best of things.) Faith, here it is. Romeo is banished...Then, since the case so stands as now it doth, I think it best you married with the County. O, he's a lovely gentleman! Romeo's a dishcloth to him! *(Juliet gasps as her old friend recommends bigamy, both a sin and a crime, but the Nurse foolishly sees only its advantages.)* Beshrew my very heart, I think you are happy in this second match, for it excels your first. Or if it did not, your first is dead — or twere as good he were, as living here and you no use of him.

Juliet: Speakest thou this from thy heart?

Nurse: And from my soul too! *(She gives the girl a hug. Juliet does not respond. She realizes now she is completely on her own, not yet fourteen but forced to think as a grown woman.)*

Juliet: Amen!

Nurse: What?

Juliet: (Pretending to agree with the Nurse, whom she now cannot trust.) Well, thou hast comforted me marvelous much. Go in, and tell my lady I am gone, having displeased my father, to Lawrence' cell, to make confession and to be absolved.

Nurse: Marry, I will, and this is wisely done.

(She leaves cheerily to tell the Capulets of Juliet's change of heart. As soon as she is gone, Juliet curses the Nurse for her double-faced suggestion, given less than an hour after Romeo has left Juliet's bed.)

Juliet: Ancient damnation! O most wicked fiend! Go, counselor! Thou and my bosom henceforth shall be twain. *(She has one last hope.)* I'll to the Friar to know his remedy. *(Slowly)* If all else fail, myself have power to die…*(With deliberation, she takes her cloak and leaves.)*

ACT IV

Scene 1

(In Friar Lawrence's cell, he and Count Paris speak of Paris's coming wedding with Juliet. The Friar tries to hide his alarm at the plans.)

Friar: On Thursday, sir? The time is very short.

Paris: My father Capulet will have it so, and I am nothing slow to slack his haste.

Friar: You say you do not know the lady's mind? *(Frowning)* I like it not!

Paris: Immoderately she weeps for Tybalt's death, and therefore have I little talked of love. Now, sir, her father counts it dangerous that she do give her sorrow so much sway, and in his wisdom hastes our marriage.

Friar: (Glancing out the window) Look, sir, here comes the lady toward my cell. *(Juliet knocks and enters in a rush. She stops short when she sees Paris, controls her surprise and curtsies to the priest.)*

Paris: Happily met, my lady and my wife!

Juliet: That may be, sir, when I "may be" a wife.

Paris: That "may be" **must** be, love, on Thursday next.

Juliet: What must be, shall be.

Friar: That's a certain text.

Paris: Come you to make confession to this father?

Juliet: To answer that, I should confess to **you.**

Paris: (Looking at her swollen eyelids.) Poor soul, thy face is much abused with tears.

Juliet: (Trying to ignore Paris politely.) Are you at leisure, holy father, now? Or shall I come to you at evening mass?

Friar: My leisure serves me, pensive daughter, now. *(Pushing Paris to the door.)* My lord, we must entreat the time alone.

Paris: Juliet, on Thursday early will I rouse ye. Till then, adieu. And keep this holy kiss. *(He kisses her lightly and leaves. She wipes off the kiss and bursts into tears.)*

Juliet: O, shut the door, and when thou has done so, come weep with me...past hope, past cure, past help!

Friar: Ah, Juliet, I already know thy grief. I hear thou must, on Thursday next, be married to this County.

Juliet: Tell me not, Friar, that thou hearest of this, unless thou tell me how I may prevent it. If, in thy wisdom, thou canst give no help,... *(She draws a dagger)*...with this knife, I'll help it presently. *(The Friar, alarmed at the suicide threat, takes the dagger from her.)* God joined my heart and Romeo's, thou our hands. *(The Friar nods thoughtfully.)* Be not so long to speak. I long to die, if what

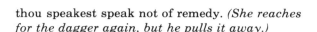

thou speakest speak not of remedy. *(She reaches for the dagger again, but he pulls it away.)*

Friar: Hold, daughter. I do spy a kind of hope. If, rather than to marry County Paris, thou hast the strength of will to slay thyself, then is it likely thou wilt undertake a thing **like** death. And, if thou darest, I'll give thee remedy.

Juliet: (Willing to take any risk.) O, bid me leap, rather than marry Paris, from off the battlements of yonder tower. Or bid me go into a new-made grave and hide me with a dead man in his shroud — things that, to hear them told, have made me tremble — and I will do it without fear or doubt, to live an unstained wife to my sweet love.

Friar: (Carefully he goes to his table where he experiments with herbs and medicines. From the bubbling retorts he siphons off liquid into a tiny vial and corks it.) Hold then. Go home, be merry, give consent to marry Paris.

Wednesday is tomorrow. Tomorrow night look that thou lie alone. *(She listens carefully.)* Let not the Nurse lie with thee in thy chamber. Take thou this vial, being then in bed, and this distilled liquor drink thou off. *(He holds the vial with the sleeping potion before her.)* When presently through all thy veins shall run a cold and drowsy humor, for no pulse shall keep his progress, no warmth, no breath shall testify thou livest. The roses in thy lips and cheeks shall fade. Each part shall, stiff and stark and cold, appear like death. And in this borrowed likeness of shrunk death,

thou shalt continue two-and-forty hours, and then awake as from a pleasant sleep.

(Describing the discovery of her "dead" body on the morrow.) Now, when the bridegroom in the morning comes to rouse thee from thy bed, there art thou "dead"! Then, as the manner of our country is, in thy best robes thou shalt be borne to that same ancient vault where all the kindred of the Capulets lie.

In the meantime, shall Romeo by my letters know our drift, and hither shall he come. And he and I will watch thy waking. And that very night shall Romeo bear thee hence to Mantua! *(Her smile grows at the happy ending of the plan, and she reaches out for the little vial of liquid.)*

Juliet: Give me, give me! O, tell not me of fear!

Friar: (Putting the little bottle into her eager hands.) Hold! Get you gone! Be strong and prosperous in this resolve. *(He turns to his writing desk.)* I'll send a friar with speed to Mantua, with my letters to thy lord.

Juliet: Love, give me strength! *(She kisses the friar's old cheek in thanks, as he starts to write a letter to Romeo.)* Farewell, dear father! *(She runs out the door happily.)*

Scene 2

(In the great hall of Capulet's house, Capulet and his wife, the Nurse, and servants are hustling about,

preparing for Juliet's wedding. Capulet gives a list of names to a servant.)

Capulet: So many guests invite as here are writ. *(To another man.)* Sirrah, go hire me twenty cunning cooks.

Servant: You shall have none ill, sir.

Capulet: Go, begone! *(The servants leave, and Capulet speaks to the Nurse.)* What, is my daughter gone to Friar Lawrence?

Nurse: Ay, forsooth.

Capulet: (Rubbing his hands with satisfaction.) Well, he may chance to do some good on her.

Nurse: (Seeing Juliet enter, radiant with smiles.) See where she comes from shrift with merry look.

Capulet: (Again the loving father as he sees she is no longer stubborn.) How now, my headstrong? Where have you been gadding?

Juliet: (Kneeling before him) Where I have learnt me to repent the sin of disobedient opposition to you, and am enjoined by holy Lawrence to beg your pardon. Pardon, I beseech you!

Capulet: (Joyfully to his wife) Send for the County! Go tell him of this! *(In happiness, he moves the time of the wedding up to the very next day, Wednesday.)* I'll have this knot knit up tomorrow morning! *(Lady Capulet looks alarmed at the idea, but Capulet bubbles with joy.)* Stand up! *(Juliet stands and he kisses her forehead.)* This is as it

should be. *(To a servant.)* Let me see the County. Ay, marry, go, I say, and fetch him hither!

Juliet: (Going to the Nurse) Nurse, will you go with me into my closet to help me sort such needful ornaments as you think fit to furnish me tomorrow?

Lady Capulet: No, not till Thursday! There is time enough.

Capulet: (Pushing Juliet and the Nurse towards her room.) Go, Nurse, go with her! *(To his wife, who scowls at the additional problems of getting all ready for such a feast.)* We'll to church tomorrow!

Lady Capulet: (Worried about the necessary food.) We shall be short in our provision. Tis now near night!

Capulet: Tush, I will stir about, and all things shall be well, I warrant thee, wife. Go thou to Juliet, help to deck up her. I'll not to bed tonight. Let me alone. *(He plans to manage all the arrangements.)* I'll play the housewife for this once. *(Calls to a servant)* What, ho! *(No one answers.)* They are all forth. Well, I will walk myself to County Paris, to prepare up him against tomorrow! *(He slaps his wife heartily on her back.)* My heart is wondrous light!

Scene 3

(In Juliet's chamber, she and the Nurse have selected a beautiful white gown, exquisite jewels, and a headdress with veil for the wedding. The room is littered

*with discarded dresses and scarves. The Nurse is all
smiles. Juliet, clad only in a simple shift, is serious.)*

Juliet: Ay, those attires are best. But, gentle Nurse, I
pray thee, leave me to myself tonight. *(Her mother
enters, vexed with the difficulties of arranging a
major celebration on short notice.)*

Lady Capulet: What, are you busy, ho? Need you my
help?

Juliet: No, madam. *(She shows the gown, and her
mother nods in approval.)* So please you, let me
now be left alone, and let the Nurse this night sit
up with you. For I am sure you have your hands
full all in this so-sudden business.

*Lady Capulet: (Surprised and pleased at the girl's
cooperation, she gives her a brisk kiss.)* Good
night. Get thee to bed and rest, for thou hast need.
*(She and the Nurse hurry off. Juliet looks after
them as the door closes, and she whispers to herself.)*

Juliet: Farewell! God knows when we shall meet again.
*(She leans against the door, drawing the little vial
from her bosom. She shudders at the sight of it.)* I
have a faint cold fear thrills through my veins that
almost freezes up the heat of life. I'll call them
back again to comfort me. *(She opens the door and
calls out.)* Nurse! *(But she shuts the door again
hurriedly.)* What should she do here? My dismal
scene I needs must act alone.

*(Putting the vial on the bedside chest, she quickly
slips on her wedding gown and headdress. Then,
slowly, she takes up the little bottle once more.)*

Come, vial! What if this mixture do not work at all?
Must I of force be married to the County? No,
no....*(She takes a dagger from the bedside chest
and puts it under her pillow.)* This shall forbid it.
Lie thou there.

*(Again she takes the vial, staring at it as she sits
on the edge of the bed, beginning to have doubts.)*
What if it be a poison which the Friar subtly hath
ministered to have me dead, lest in this marriage
he should be dishonored because he married me
before to Romeo? I fear it is. And yet, methinks it
should not, for he hath still been tried a holy man.

*(She starts to drink the liquid, but a grisly thought
stops her.)* How if, when I am laid into the tomb, I
wake before the time that Romeo come to redeem
me? There's a fearful point! Shall I not then be
stifled in the vault, to whose foul mouth no health-
some air breathes in, and there die strangled ere
my Romeo comes?

*(An even worse thought comes — not suffocation,
but madness.)* Or, if I live, is it not very like — the
horrible conceit of death and night, together with
the terror of the place — as in a vault, an ancient
receptacle where, for this many hundred years, the
bones of all my buried ancestors are packed; where
bloody Tybalt, yet but green in earth, lies festering
in his shroud; where, as they say, at some hours in
the night spirits resort....alack, alack, is it not like
that I, so early waking — what with loathsome
smells and shrieks that living mortals, hearing

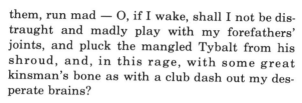

them, run mad — O, if I wake, shall I not be dis-
traught and madly play with my forefathers'
joints, and pluck the mangled Tybalt from his
shroud, and, in this rage, with some great
kinsman's bone as with a club dash out my desperate brains?

*(To her over-wrought imagination, she already
sees the spirit of dead Tybalt walking.)* O, look!
Methinks I see my cousin's ghost seeking out
Romeo, that did spit his body upon a rapier's
point. *(She puts out her hands to ward off the
ghost.)* Stay, Tybalt, stay!

*(She collapses on her bed, sobbing, and lifts the
vial to her lips.)* Romeo, I come! This do I drink to
thee! *(She drinks and slowly sinks on the pillow,
her wedding gown and veil spread wide about her.
As she drowses off, she pulls the bed-curtain half-
closed.)*

Scene 4

*(In the main hall, all rush about putting up the last
decorations for the wedding. Outside, a cock crows,
though stars still shine. Lady Capulet gives her ring of
great household keys to the Nurse.)*

Lady Capulet: Hold, take these keys and fetch more
spices, Nurse.

Nurse: They call for dates and quinces in the pastry.

Capulet: (Entering, he scolds the servants in happy fashion.) Come, stir, stir, stir! The second cock hath crowed, the curfew bell hath rung, tis three o'clock. *(To the Nurse)* Look to the baked meats, good Angelica. Spare not for cost!

Nurse: (As a joke, she calls him a male housewife.) Go, you cot-quean, go, get you to bed! Faith, you'll be sick tomorrow for this night's watching!

Capulet: No, not a whit. What, I have watched ere now all night for lesser cause, and never been sick. *(The Nurse and Lady Capulet leave, as servants enter with spits for roast meat, together with logs and baskets.)* Now, fellow, what is there?

First Servant: Things for the cook, sir, but I know not what.

Capulet: (Waving him towards the kitchen.) Make haste, make haste. *(As the First Servant leaves, Capulet speaks to a Second Servant.)* Sirrah, fetch drier logs. Call Peter. He will show thee where they are. *(The Second Servant leaves. Capulet goes to the window, where the sky lightens.)* Good faith, tis day. The County will be here with music straight, for so he said he would. *(Merry music floats through the window.)* I hear him near. *(He calls.)* Nurse! Wife! What ho! What, Nurse, I say! *(The Nurse enters, all smiles.)* Go waken Juliet. Go and trim her up! I'll go and chat with Paris. Hie, make haste, make haste! The bridegroom, he is come already! Make haste, I say! *(The Nurse scurries off, clasping her hands with excitement, and Capulet laughs happily.)*

Scene 5

(In Juliet's chamber, the Nurse enters and draws the window curtains, letting in the first rays of the sun. With a happy, teasing voice, she scolds Juliet for oversleeping.)

Nurse: Mistress! What, mistress! Juliet! *(She shakes her head at such sound sleep.)* Fast, I warrant her, she. *(Calls again)* Why, lamb! Why, lady! Fie, you slugabed. *(She picks up various discarded gowns lying about and tidies the room as she continues to call.)* Why, love, I say! Madam! Sweetheart! Why, bride...what, not a word? *(She shrugs with an earthy laugh.)* Sleep for a week — for the **next** night, I warrant, the County Paris hath set up his rest, that you shall rest but little! *(Crosses herself for her naughtiness.)* God forgive me, marry and amen!

(She goes to the bed curiously.) How sound is she asleep! I must needs wake her. *(She calls at the half-closed bed-curtain.)* Madam, madam, madam! *(She draws the curtain aside.)* What, dressed, and in your clothes, and down again? I must needs wake you. Lady! *(She shakes her. She shakes her again. With growing horror, the Nurse shakes Juliet again and cries out shrilly.)* Lady! Lady! Alas, alas! — Help, help! My lady's...dead! *(She rushes to the door, screaming for brandy and help.)* Some aqua-vitae, ho! My lord! My lady!

Lady Capulet: (Entering, alarmed. She carries a bunch of rosemary, the flower of remembrance, to be used in the wedding.) What noise is here?

Nurse: O lamentable day!

Lady Capulet: What is the matter?

Nurse: (Pointing to the bed) Look, look! O heavy day! *(She bursts into tears and moans.)*

Lady Capulet: (Running to the bed and taking Juliet in her arms, with a rush of motherhood.) O me, O me! My child, my only life! *(She shakes her gently.)* Revive, look up, or I will die with thee! *(Calling out)* Help, help! Call help!

Capulet: (Entering with a broad grin as jolly music strikes up behind him.) For shame, bring Juliet forth. Her lord is come!

Nurse: She's dead. Deceased. She's dead, alack the day!

Lady Capulet: Alack the day, she's dead, she's dead, she's dead!

Capulet: (Stunned, he brushes them all aside and stoops to take Juliet's wrist.) Ha! Let me see her. Out, alas! She's cold, her blood is settled, and her joints are stiff. *(He kisses his daughter with awkward gentleness as he speaks slowly.)* Death lies on her like an untimely frost upon the sweetest flower of all the field.

Nurse: O lamentable day!

Lady Capulet: O woeful time!

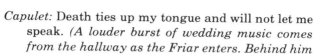

Capulet: Death ties up my tongue and will not let me speak. *(A louder burst of wedding music comes from the hallway as the Friar enters. Behind him comes a smiling Paris, holding wedding flowers and rosemary in his hands.)*

Friar: Come, is the bride ready to go to church?

Capulet: Ready to go, but never to return. *(As the joyful music falters and dies, Capulet speaks to Paris.)* O son, the night before thy wedding day hath Death lain with thy wife. There she lies. Death is my son-in-law. Death is my heir. My daughter he hath wedded. I will die and leave him all. Life, living — all is Death's.

Paris: (Going to Juliet, he stands in amazement and sorrow by her bed.) Have I thought long to see this morning's face, and doth it give me such a sight as this?

Lady Capulet: Accursed, unhappy, wretched, hateful day! But one, poor one, one poor and loving child, and cruel Death hath catched it from my sight.

Nurse: O woe! O woeful, woeful, woeful day!

Friar: (Giving the comfort of religion, that Juliet is in Heaven.) Peace, ho, for shame! Confusion's cure lives not in these confusions. Heaven and yourself had part in this fair maid — now Heaven hath all. And all the better is it for the maid. And weep ye now, seeing she is advanced above the clouds, as high as Heaven itself? Dry up your tears and stick your rosemary on this fair corpse, and as the custom is, all in her best array, bear her to church.

Capulet: *(Giving sad orders to the household.)* All things that we ordained festival...turn from their office to black funeral: our instruments to melancholy bells, our wedding cheer to a sad burial feast, our bridal flowers serve for a burial corpse, and all things change them to the contrary.

Friar: *(Urging Capulet back to the main hall.)* Sir, go you in. And madam, go with him. And go, Sir Paris. Everyone prepare to follow this fair corpse unto her grave. *(They sadly strew Juliet's body with sprigs of rosemary and leave the Friar to give the last rites to the corpse. Hurriedly he removes the vial from her sleeping hand.)*

ACT V

Scene 1

(In the neighboring town of Mantua, Romeo waits for news, feeling lighthearted because of a dream he has had the night before.)

Romeo: If I may trust the flattering eye of sleep, my dreams presage some joyful news at hand. My bosom's lord sits lightly in his throne! And all this day an unaccustomed spirit lifts me above the ground with cheerful thoughts. I dreamt my lady came and found me dead — strange dream that gives a dead man leave to think! — and breathed such life with kisses in my lips that I revived and was an Emperor! *(His servant, Balthasar, enters, wearing riding boots, as he has just come from Verona. Romeo rushes to greet him, but the servant can hardly look him in the eye.)* News from Verona! — How now, Balthasar? Dost thou not bring me letters from the Friar? How doth my lady? Is my father well? How fares my Juliet? That I ask again, for nothing can be ill if she be well.

Balthasar: *(Sadly)* Then she is well, and nothing can be ill. *(He makes the Sign of the Cross, as he has just witnessed her funeral.)* Her body sleeps in Capel's monument, and her immortal part with angels lives. *(Romeo stands silent and stunned at*

❁≈≈≈≈≈≈≈≈≈≈≈≈≈≈≈≈≈≈≈≈≈≈≈≈≈≈≈❁

the news. Balthasar breaks into harsh sobs.) O, pardon me for bringing these ill news!

Romeo: (Slowly) Is it even so? *(He cries out in challenge to the sky.)* Then I defy you, stars! *(To Balthasar, with unusual quietness.)* Thou knowest my lodging. Get me ink and paper, and hire post horses. I will hence tonight.

Balthasar: (Alarmed at his master's odd manner, he curbs his own tears.) I do beseech you, sir, have patience. Your looks are pale and wild.

Romeo: Tush, thou art deceived. Leave me, and do the thing I bid thee do. *(Desperately)* Hast thou no letters to me from the Friar?

Balthasar: No, my good lord.

Romeo: No matter. Get thee gone and hire those horses. I'll be with thee straight.

(The servant leaves. Romeo stands, no longer a sobbing youth in love, but a man full-grown in hopeless grief. He makes a quiet pledge.) Well, Juliet, I will lie with thee tonight. *(Calmly he plans to join her in death.)* Let's see for means. O mischief, thou art swift to enter in the thoughts of desperate men!

(He recalls a poverty-stricken drug-seller nearby.) I do remember an apothecary, and hereabouts he dwells. Sharp misery had worn him to the bones. And in his needy shop a tortoise hung, an alligator stuffed, and other skins of ill-shaped fishes. And about his shelves, a beggarly account of empty

boxes, green earthen pots, bladders, and musty seeds, remnants of packthread, and old cakes of roses were thinly scattered, to make up a show. To myself I said, "And if a man did need a poison now, whose sale is present death in Mantua, here lives a wretch would sell it him." And this same needy man must sell it me. *(He approaches a shop.)* As I remember, this should be the house. What, ho! Apothecary!

Apothecary: (Appearing at his door, a ragged starved man.) Who calls so loud?

Romeo: Come hither, man. I see that thou art poor. Hold...*(He shows a handful of gold.)*...there is forty ducats. Let me have a dram of poison.

Apothecary: (Looking about uneasily for witnesses.) Such mortal drugs I have, but Mantua's law is death to any he that utters them.

Romeo: Famine is in thy cheeks. The world is not thy friend, nor the world's law. The world affords no law to make thee rich. Then be not poor, but break it and take this.

Apothecary: (His hand reaches for the gold while he shakes his head unwillingly.) My poverty, but not my will, consents.

Romeo: I pay thy poverty and not thy will.

Apothecary: (Going into his shop and returning instantly with a small vial.) Put this in any liquid thing you will, and drink it off. And if you had the strength of twenty men, it would dispatch you straight.

Romeo: There is thy gold. *(He puts the coins into the skinny hand.)* Farewell. Buy food and get thyself in flesh. *(To the little bottle, as if it were a sweet drink.)* Come, cordial and not poison, go with me to Juliet's grave, for there must I use thee.

Scene 2

(In Friar Lawrence's cell, a younger priest, Friar John, rushes in, travel-stained and upset.)

John: Holy Franciscan Friar, brother, ho!

Friar Lawrence: Friar John, welcome from Mantua. What says Romeo? Or, if his mind be writ, give me his letter.

John: (Unhappily telling how, on the way out of Verona, he entered a plague-stricken house to find his traveling companion, and they were both locked in the place.) Going to find a barefoot brother out, one of our order, to associate me, here in this city visiting the sick, and finding him — the searchers of the town, suspecting that we both were in a house where the infectious pestilence did reign, sealed up the doors and would not let us forth.

Friar Lawrence: Who bore my letter, then, to Romeo?

John: I could not send it. *(He draws forth Friar Lawrence's letter to Romeo and returns it.)* Here it is again.

Friar Lawrence: (Alarmed) Unhappy fortune! By my brotherhood, the letter was of dear import, and the neglecting it may do much danger. *(He realizes he must pry open Juliet's tomb alone.)* Friar John, go hence. Get me an iron crow and bring it straight unto my cell.

John: Brother, I'll go and bring it thee. *(He leaves to fetch the crowbar.)*

Friar Lawrence: Now must I to the monument alone. Within this three hours will fair Juliet wake. But I will write again to Mantua and keep her at my cell till Romeo come. Poor living corpse, closed in a dead man's tomb!

Scene 3

(Night has fallen, and in the churchyard before the great marble family tomb of the Capulets, young Paris visits his bride's grave. With him in the dark is his Page, carrying a torch and flowers for the tomb.)

Paris: Give me thy torch, boy. Hence, and stand aloof. Yet put it out, for I would not be seen. *(The boy rubs the torch out in the dirt, as Paris tells him to stand watch.)* Under yon yew trees lay thee all along, holding thine ear close to the hollow ground. So shall no foot upon the churchyard tread but thou shalt hear it. Whistle then to me, as signal that thou hearest something approach. Give me those flowers. Do as I bid thee, go.

Page: (To himself) I am almost afraid to stand alone here in the churchyard. *(He leaves nervously, looking about for ghosts.)*

Paris: (Putting the flowers before the bronze doors of the tomb.) Sweet flower, with flowers thy bridal bed I strew. O woe! Thy canopy is dust and stones. *(The Page whistles a signal.)* The boy gives warning something doth approach. *(He sees a flickering light)* What, with a torch? *(He hides in the shadows.)* Muffle me, night, awhile. *(Romeo enters with his man, Balthasar, who carries a torch, a pick-mattock, and an iron crowbar.)*

Romeo: Give me that mattock and the wrenching iron. *(He gives Balthasar a note in return.)* Hold, take this letter. Early in the morning see thou deliver it to my lord and father. Give me the light. Upon thy life I charge thee — whatever thou hearest or seest, stand all aloof and do not interrupt me in my course! Therefore hence, be gone!

Balthasar: (Obediently) I will be gone, sir, and not trouble you.

Romeo: So shalt thou show me friendship. *(He gives him a purse of gold.)* Take thou that. Live, and be prosperous. And farewell, good fellow.

Balthasar: (Aside to himself) For all this same, I'll hide me hereabout. His looks I fear, and his intents I doubt. *(Pretending to leave, he also hides in the churchyard and watches, as Romeo pries open the great doors to the tomb with his crowbar.)*

Romeo: Thou womb of death, thus I enforce thy rotten jaws to open. I'll cram thee with more food! *(The doors groan and the hinges give. Romeo drags the doors open, as Paris watches, thinking Romeo is vandalizing the tomb to continue the feud.)*

Paris: This is that banished haughty Montague that murdered my love's cousin — with which grief it is supposed the fair creature died — and here is come to do some villainous shame to the dead bodies. *(He steps out of the shadows into the light of Romeo's torch and shouts.)* Stop, vile Montague! *(As a noble, he arrests Romeo.)* Condemned villain, I do apprehend thee. Obey, and go with me, for thou must die!

Romeo: I must indeed, and therefore came I hither. *(Kindly he tries to avoid a fight.)* Good gentle youth, tempt not a desperate man! Fly hence and leave me. I beseech thee, youth, put not another sin upon my head by urging me to fury. *(Paris draws his sword.)* Stay not! Be gone! Live, and hereafter say, a madman's mercy bid thee run away.

Paris: (Determined to arrest Romeo) I do defy thy conjurations and apprehend thee for a felon here. *(He thrusts his sword at Romeo.)*

Romeo: Wilt thou provoke me? Then have at thee, boy! *(He draws his sword and they fight furiously in the torchlit darkness.)*

Page: O Lord, they fight! I will go call the watch. *(As the Page leaves, Paris falls, wounded to death by Romeo's quick blade.)*

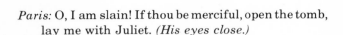

Paris: O, I am slain! If thou be merciful, open the tomb, lay me with Juliet. *(His eyes close.)*

Romeo: In faith, I will! *(He takes the torch and holds it close to see whom he has killed.)* Mercutio's kinsman, noble County Paris! *(With bewildered remembrance)* What said my man? I think he told me Paris should have married Juliet. Said he not so, or did I dream it so? Or am I mad, hearing him talk of Juliet, to think it was so? *(To the dead youth, with friendship.)* O give me thy hand, one writ with me in sour Misfortune's book! *(A promise to his dead new friend.)* I'll bury thee in a triumphant grave!

(He opens wide the doors of the tomb to show Juliet, lying on her marble coffin, and he places Paris reverently on the floor at her feet. Then he approaches his young bride, her face covered with her wedding veil. He lifts the gossamer and folds it back to look upon her face again.) O my love, my wife! Death, that hath sucked the honey of thy breath, hath had no power yet upon thy beauty. Thou art not conquered.

(He goes further into the vault, where other dead repose. At one bier he stops to speak to the young man he has killed.) Tybalt, liest thou there in thy bloody sheet? Forgive me, cousin!

(Returning to his beautiful young wife, whom Death perhaps has stolen to be his mistress.) Ah, dear Juliet, why art thou yet so fair? Shall I believe that unsubstantial Death is amorous, and that the lean, abhorred monster keeps thee here in dark to be his paramour? *(He vows never to leave her*

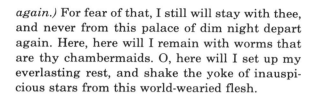

again.) For fear of that, I still will stay with thee, and never from this palace of dim night depart again. Here, here will I remain with worms that are thy chambermaids. O, here will I set up my everlasting rest, and shake the yoke of inauspicious stars from this world-wearied flesh.

Eyes, look your last! *(He holds her slender form to his heart.)* Arms, take your last embrace. And lips, O you the doors of breath, seal with a righteous kiss a dateless bargain to engrossing death!

(Tenderly he kisses Juliet for the last time. And then, almost with joy, he takes the vial of poison and holds it up, as in a toast.) Here's to my love! *(He drinks, and instantly the poison begins to work.)* O true Apothecary! Thy drugs are quick. Thus with a kiss I die! *(He kisses her, but his arms begin to slide away, and he falls to the floor. For a moment all is still. Juliet's hand moves a little and lies again at rest. Into the dark bobs a lantern light held by Friar Lawrence, who carries a crowbar and a spade.)*

Friar: Saint Francis be my speed! How oft tonight have my old feet stumbled at graves. *(Hearing a noise, he stops.)* Who's there?

Balthasar: (Coming from the shadows) Here's one, a friend, and one that knows you well.

Friar: Bliss be upon you! Tell me, good my friend, what torch is yond? As I discern, it burneth in the Capels' monument.

Balthasar: It doth so, holy sir. And there's my master, one that you love.

Friar: (Alarmed) Who is it?

Balthasar: Romeo.

Friar: How long hath he been there?

Balthasar: Full half an hour.

Friar: Go with me to the vault.

Balthasar: I dare not, sir. My master fearfully did menace me with death if I did stay to look.

Friar: Stay then. I'll go alone. *(He shudders.)* Fear comes upon me.

Balthasar: As I did sleep under this yew tree here, I dreamt my master and another fought, and that my master slew him.

Friar: (Calling) Romeo! *(At the door of the tomb he pauses and looks at the pavement.)* Alack, alack, what blood is this which stains the stony entrance of this sepulchre? What mean these swords? *(He enters the gates of the dark tomb and bends over Romeo's body.)* Romeo! O, pale! *(He looks at the foot of Juliet's tomb.)* Who else? What, Paris too? And steeped in blood? Ah, what an unkind hour! *(He straightens up as Juliet moves slowly.)* The lady stirs!

Juliet: (Rising a little, still dazed from sleep, she props herself on her elbow. When she sees the Friar, she smiles in gratitude.) O comfortable Friar! Where is my lord? I do remember well where I should be, and there I am. Where is my Romeo?

Friar: (As the armor of the town watchmen clangs and their lights appear in the distance.) I hear some noise. Lady, come from that nest of death. Come, come away!

(She refuses, confused, until he points in sorrow at Romeo's body.) Thy husband in thy bosom there lies dead. And Paris too. *(She shakes her head in denial, unable to believe the sight at first. Then the loss of her young husband grows within her, and she draws in her breath sharply, as the old Friar continues.)* Stay not to question, for the watch is coming. Come, go, good Juliet! *(Trembling with fear and old age.)* I dare no longer stay!

Juliet: (To the Friar) Go, get thee hence, for I will not away. *(The aged priest, quivering with shock, hurries off. Juliet slowly rises from the coffin and bends over Romeo, knowing all is lost. She takes his hand and opens his fingers.)*

What's here? A cup, closed in my true-love's hand? Poison, I see, hath been his timeless end. *(She raises the vial to her lips, but it is empty. With love she chides Romeo for drinking all of it.)* O churl! Drunk all and left no friendly drop to help me after? I will kiss thy lips. Haply some poison yet doth hang on them to make me die with a restorative.

(She kisses him and draws back in fresh grief, with the realization he has died only moments before.) Thy lips are warm!

1 Watchman: (Calling in the distance) Lead, boy. Which way?

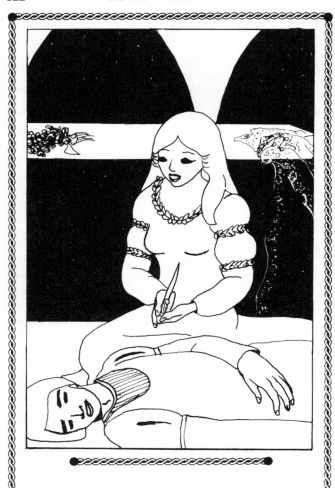

Juliet: O happy dagger! This is thy sheath
— there rust, and let me die....

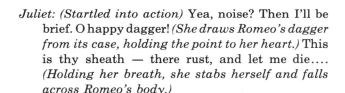

Juliet: (Startled into action) Yea, noise? Then I'll be brief. O happy dagger! *(She draws Romeo's dagger from its case, holding the point to her heart.)* This is thy sheath — there rust, and let me die.... *(Holding her breath, she stabs herself and falls across Romeo's body.)*

Page: (Entering with the Watchmen.) This is the place. There, where the torch doth burn.

1 Watchman: The ground is bloody. Search about the churchyard. *(As some leave, he catches sight of the dead in the tomb.)* Pitiful sight! Here lies the County slain! And Juliet bleeding, warm, and newly dead, who here hath lain this two days buried. Go, tell the Prince! Run to the Capulets! Raise up the Montagues. Some others search! *(As his men leave, others return with Romeo's servant, Balthasar.)*

2 Watchman: Here's Romeo's man. We found him in the churchyard.

1 Watchman: Hold him in safety till the Prince come hither. *(As he speaks, another Watchman enters with Friar Lawrence.)*

3 Watchman: Here is a friar that trembles, sighs, and weeps. We took this mattock and this spade from him as he was coming from this churchyard's side.

1 Watchman: A great suspicion! Stay the friar too.

Prince: (Entering with some noblemen) What misadventure is so early up that calls our person from our morning rest?

Capulet: (Entering with his wife and others.) What should it be, that is so shrieked abroad?

Lady Capulet: The people in the street cry "Romeo," some "Juliet," and some "Paris." And all run with open outcry toward our monument.

1 Watchman: Sovereign, here lies the County Paris slain, and Romeo dead, and Juliet, dead before, warm and new-killed.

Capulet: O Heavens! O wife, look how our daughter bleeds! *(He is overcome at the sight.)*

Lady Capulet: (Kneeling, she feels her own death coming soon.) O me, this sight of death is as a bell that warns my old age to a sepulchre!

Prince: (As Montague enters, dressed in black mourning.) Come, Montague, for thou art early up to see thy son and heir more early down.

Montague: Alas, my liege, my wife is dead tonight! Grief of my son's exile hath stopped her breath. What further woe conspires against mine age?

Prince: (Pointing to the tomb) Look, and thou shalt see.

Montague: (Kneeling over Romeo, protesting his haste in dying before his father.) O thou untaught! What manners is in this — to press before thy father to a grave?

Prince: (Motioning for quiet) Seal up the mouth of outrage for a while. *(To the Watchmen)* Bring forth the parties of suspicion.

Friar: I am the greatest. *(He shakes from guilt and grief.)*

Prince: Then say at once what thou dost know in this.

Friar: I will be brief. Romeo, there dead, was husband to that Juliet. I married them, and their stolen marriage day was Tybalt's doomsday. *(To Old Capulet)* You would have married her perforce to County Paris. Then gave I her a sleeping potion. Meantime I writ to Romeo that he should hither come, but he which bore my letter, Friar John, was stayed by accident. But when I came, some minute ere the time of her awaking, here untimely lay the noble Paris and true Romeo dead. She wakes, and I entreated her come forth, but then a noise did scare me from the tomb. And she, too desperate, would not go with me. If aught in this miscarried by my fault, let my old life be sacrificed. *(He weeps in despair.)*

Prince: (Kindly) We still have known thee for a holy man. *(To the parents)* Where be these enemies? Capulet, Montague, see what a scourge is laid upon your hate, that Heaven finds means to kill your joys with love. *(He blames not only them but himself for not stopping the feud more firmly.)* And I, for winking at your discords too, have lost a brace of kinsmen. *(He sighs for his cousins, Mercutio and Paris.)* All are punished.

Capulet: (Extending an old hand to his enemy Montague.) O brother Montague, give my thy hand. No more can I demand.

Montague: (Clasping hands to swear peace, in memory of their lost children.) But I can give thee more.

For I will raise her statue in pure gold, that while Verona by that name is known, there shall no figure at such rate be set as that of true and faithful Juliet.

Capulet: As rich shall Romeo's by his lady's lie — poor sacrifices of our enmity. *(They weep together, thinking of the two statues, all that will be left of their children.)*

Prince: (Gazing at the gray light of early dawn.) A glooming peace this morning with it brings. The sun for sorrow will not show his head. Go hence, to have more talk of these sad things. Some shall be pardoned, and some punished. For never was a story of more woe than this of Juliet and her Romeo.

FINIS

SOME FAMOUS QUOTATIONS

Chorus: ...a pair of star-crossed lovers...the two hours' traffic of our stage. *(Act I, Scene 1)*

Romeo: He that is strucken blind cannot forget the precious treasure of his eyesight lost. *(Act I, Scene 1)*

Peter: I must to the learned! *(Act I, Scene 2)*

Peter: I pray come and crush a cup of wine! *(Act I, Scene 2)*

Benvolio: I will make thee think thy "swan" a crow! *(Act I, Scene 2)*

Mercutio: O, then I see Queen Mab hath been with you! *(Act I, Scene 4)*

Romeo: O, she doth teach the torches to burn bright! It seems she hangs upon the cheek of night like a rich jewel in an Ethiop's ear — beauty too rich for use, for earth too dear! *(Act I, Scene 5)*

Romeo: He jests at scars that never felt a wound... But soft, what light through yonder window breaks? It is the East, and Juliet is the sun!...O, that I were a glove upon that hand, that I might touch that cheek! *(Act II, Scene 2)*

Juliet: O Romeo, Romeo! Wherefore art thou "Romeo"? *(Act II, Scene 2)*

Juliet: That which we call a "rose" by any other name would smell as sweet. *(Act II, Scene 2)*

Juliet: O swear not by the moon, the inconstant moon, that monthly changes in her circled orb, lest that thy love prove likewise variable! *(Act II, Scene 2)*

Romeo: How silver-sweet sound lovers' tongues by night, like softest music to attending ears! *(Act II, Scene 2)*

Juliet: Good night, good night! Parting is such sweet sorrow that I shall say, "Good night," till it be morrow. *(Act II, Scene 2)*

Friar: Virtue itself turns vice, being misapplied. And vice sometime's by action dignified. *(Act II, Scene 3)*

Mercutio: Ask for me tomorrow, and you shall find me a "grave" man...A plague on both your houses! *(Act III, Scene 1)*

Romeo: O, I am Fortune's fool! *(Act III, Scene 1)*

Juliet: Gallop apace, you fiery-footed steeds! *(Act III, Scene 2)*

Romeo: Night's candles are burnt out, and jocund day stands tiptoe on the misty mountaintops. I must be gone and live, or stay and die. *(Act III, Scene 5)*

Romeo: Dry sorrow drinks our blood. *(Act III, Scene 5)*

Juliet: O Fortune, Fortune! All men call thee fickle. **Be** fickle, Fortune, for then I hope thou wilt not keep him long, but send him back. *(Act III, Scene 5)*

Capulet: Thank me no thankings nor proud me no prouds! *(Act III, Scene 5)*

Juliet: ...come weep with me...past hope, past cure, past help! *(Act IV, Scene 1)*

Capulet: Look to the baked meats, good Angelica! Spare not for cost! *(Act IV, Scene 4)*

Capulet: Death lies on her like an untimely frost upon the sweetest flower of all the field. *(Act IV, Scene 5)*

Capulet: Death ties up my tongue and will not let me speak. *(Act IV, Scene 5)*

Apothecary: My poverty, but not my will, consents. *(Act V, Scene 1)*

Romeo: Good gentle youth, tempt not a desperate man! *(Act V, Scene 3)*

Romeo: O give me thy hand, one writ with me in sour Misfortune's book! *(Act V, Scene 3)*

Romeo: Ah, dear Juliet, why art thou yet so fair?...O, here will I set up my everlasting rest, and shake the yoke of inauspicious stars from this world-wearied flesh. *(Act V, Scene 3)*